D0891429

# Don't Say That Name!

## SanDee Stone

**Milton Publishing Company, Inc.**
Post Office Box 6
Lookout Mountain, Tennessee 37350

## Dedication

mentor\ n:  an experienced and trusted friend and adviser; someone close to you who shares your feelings, guides you, encourages you.

**This book is dedicated to my husband, Jim, who exemplifies the word, mentor, in my life.**

## Acknowledgments

My deepest gratitude goes to the many people along the way who have influenced the writing of this book.

Twenty years ago, Dr. Irv Baker encouraged me to write for 10 minutes a day. Without that advice, I would never have been able to recall all the details. The journals, scraps of papers with notes, and talks I've given throughout the years are a result of Irv's suggestion.

With many false starts, I never thought a book would be brought to fruition, but my husband, Jim, never lost hope that someday it would be accomplished.

Thank you to all the people who heard me speak throughout the years and asked to hear "the rest of the story."

My heartfelt appreciation goes to the many Gideons throughout the country who have heard my story and have retold it to the glory of God. I particularly thank Hank and Janet DeVries who started me speaking for this ministry in 1985. Also, Kenneth Speakman at the headquarters of The Gideons International in Nashville, Tennessee, who was instrumental in this book becoming a reality.

Lastly, thank you to my friend, Phyllis Neal, C. Stephen Byrum, Ph.D., Herman Heacker, publisher, and Carol Martin for their editing assistance. They allowed the story to be written as it happened, and I appreciate that immensely.

# Table of Contents

## Introduction

Life is a road, a pathway. We cannot see its beginning. It starts before we are born, while we are being formed in our mother's womb. *"You saw me before I was born and scheduled each day of my life before I began to breathe"* (Psalm 139:16 LB).

We cannot see its end; it goes on forever. As children of God, we have that assurance. *"Surely goodness and mercy shall follow me all the days of my life and I will dwell in the house of the Lord forever"* (Psalm 23:6).

Knowing this, I find no choice but to obey the admonition, *"Trust in the Lord with all your heart and lean not unto your own understanding. In all your ways acknowledge Him, and He shall direct your paths"* (Proverbs 3:5,6).

This book is written to take you on the path of life I have walked thus far. My desire is to share what I have experienced and learned about **THAT NAME,** as I've *acknowledged Him in all my ways.*

## Chapter One

### Acknowledging Him as Savior

*"Behold the Lamb of God, who taketh away the sin of the world"* (John 1:29b).

**Hartford, Connecticut 1948**

On a snowy December night, I stood shivering with cold and delight. The swirling flakes of snow and the gleaming Christmas lights on the big veranda of the Hartford Times newspaper building were a sight to behold. A choir stood poised next to an organ. A group of people had gathered in hushed expectancy and were waiting in the courtyard below. The annual Christmas carol sing was about to begin.

Suddenly, the organ music pealed into the frosty air, and the choir began to sing "Away in a Manger." My ten-year-old heart swelled with awe, and I spontaneously joined in singing with the throng. My mother, standing very close to me in the crowd, leaned over and whispered loudly in my ear, "Sing, but DON'T SAY THAT NAME! Hum when you get to it."

How could I help but wonder, *What would* happen if I said THAT NAME? *Who was this baby sung about and celebrated at this time of the year?* And most of all I wondered, *What is a little Jewish girl like me doing in a place like this anyway?*

Nine more Christmases were to come and go before I had the answers to those questions, but that night a search was begun. My heart was never at peace until I knew who that baby in the manger was and what would happen if I said his name.

*"If you seek me, you will find me, if you search with your whole heart"* (Jeremiah 29:13).

I was raised in a very Jewish environment, so the only time I thought about the questions was during the Christmas season. In the public schools I attended, we'd sing Christmas carols, but I'd obediently hum when I got to THAT NAME. I was afraid not to!

When I was a child, Christmas was a mystical time for me. It centered around that chubby old man in a red suit with a snowy white beard, twinkling eyes, reindeer that flew, and most importantly, a bag full of toys for good little girls and boys. I knew all about Santa Claus. Every department store had a "Santa's helper." Of course, the *real* Santa Claus lived at the North Pole and was very busy preparing for that wonderful Christmas eve ride. At that time, he'd distribute the gifts he and his elves had worked on all year.

Strange as it may seem, I knew more about the myth of Santa Claus than the true story of Hanukkah and the Maccabees. Hanukkah fell during the same approximate season as Christmas, but my recollection of this Jewish holiday is vague. We lit eight candles, one each night after sundown, in a candelabra called a menorah. The candles were lit to commemorate a miracle that took place in 168-165 B.C. The Maccabean warriors had reconquered the Holy City, Jerusalem. When they entered the Temple, they found that the oil used for the daily lighting of the candelabrum had been desecrated by the enemy. There was only one small, sealed jar of oil to be found. This was enough for only one day. That one small jar of oil lasted for eight days, until fresh, pure oil could be prepared. Rather than remembering the significance of the holiday, I remember that we received Hanukkah *gelt* (money) and little chocolate candies wrapped in gold foil to look like coins. We also ate potato *latkes* (pancakes). I'm sure there were reasons for these traditional practices, but to this day, I still don't know what they are. Hanukkah wasn't nearly as memorable as Christmas!

As a child growing up in an immigrant home, my mother hadn't received gifts for any occasion. She saw Christmas as a chance to shower my brother and me with everything we had mentioned wanting all year. It was a very unconventional thing for a Jewish family to do, but rules were altered to make Christmas acceptable for our family. We didn't have a Christmas tree, as that was considered a Gentile practice. We could, however, dream of a white Christmas as we listened to Bing Crosby sing, and read "The Night Before Christmas" as we waited eagerly for Santa's impending visit.

Then, that magical night came. I lovingly placed a plateful of cookies and a glass of milk on the kitchen table and climbed into bed in wild anticipation of the morning to come. I tried in vain to drift off to sleep but kept my eyes tightly shut. I was told that Santa would bypass our house if he found me awake when I heard the sleigh bells ring. And ring they did! (Of course it was my mother shaking a string of bells!)

Before sunup, my brother and I sneaked into the living room and beheld the wondrous sight of gifts piled in one area of the living room for him and in another for me. They were never wrapped because Santa doesn't have time to wrap all those gifts. So, our eyes beheld everything at once, in all their splendor. The doll I had been wanting, skates, my brother's bike, books and games - all there for us to enjoy, thanks to a benevolent Santa who came in spite of our not having a chimney for him to climb down! Who could possibly need a Christmas tree with all of this!

Until I was ten, I had never been confronted with the option of Christmas centering around anyone but Santa Claus. Now I was too old to really believe in him, yet young enough to be afraid the gifts might end if I didn't. I guardedly told my parents that I thought Santa wasn't real. Mom confessed that it was my parents' generosity blessing us all these years; therefore, the gifts would continue!

### Yom Kippur, the Day of Atonement 1950

The synagogue was slightly warm, and I was getting drowsy. Sitting in the balcony with the women and listening to the rabbi in the sanctuary below was terribly boring. Men and women were segregated in this, an Orthodox synagogue, and I wondered why. The rabbi droned on in Hebrew, and for a while I tried to follow along in the prayer book. On one side of the page, the text was in Hebrew; on the other, English.

As my mind wandered, I wondered about other things. *Why were we taught to merely read Hebrew and not translate so that we could understand?* I wondered, *What would happen if I died before being able to fast next year.* I wondered about sin and atonement. So many questions; so few answers.

Putting aside my beginnings of questions about the ancient religion into which I had been born, I quietly slid from my seat and went in search of diversion.

At the foot of the balcony stairs, I ran into my friend Irwin, also looking for an escape. "Let's go over to my house," he suggested. Since he lived just across the street, I quickly agreed.

The front door opened into the living room and my young mind reeled in shock at the scene before me. There was Irwin's father and some of the leaders of the synagogue in front of the blaring TV. They munched on pretzels and guzzled beer as they watched the 1950 World's Series. The Yankees were playing the Phillies, and the men cheered for their favorite team. Something in me died that day, and they didn't even know it.

Yom Kippur, the Day of Atonement - the day to get right with God. From earliest childhood I understood that my only access to forgiveness was totally fasting on this one day a year, and I took it very seriously. I knew I was a sinner. One of the verses in the prayer book I had read in English was found in **Deuteronomy 6:5**, *"Thou shalt love the Lord thy God with all thine heart, and with all thy soul, and with all thy might."* I knew I didn't love God *that* much. If I were honest, I loved my mom and dad, my kid brother, and most of all, myself. God definitely wasn't first. I lived with the hope that I'd survive until next Yom Kippur and with the fear that I might not.

My teen years sometimes found me pondering about God, the emptiness of the synagogue service rituals, the senselessness of an ancient language that I could read but not translate, and the futile effort to pray to a God who was somewhere off in the clouds. Yet, in spite of all this, I believed He existed.

I asked about the Old Testament sacrifice of a lamb for a sin offering and was told that this could not happen today because the temple in Jerusalem had been destroyed. *What kind of God would give us access to Him and then take it away?* Questions, questions! Still no answers. "Fast and pray on Yom Kippur, and stop asking so many questions," I was told. But the questions were there!

No one I knew really followed the rules and  regulations that were written in the scriptures, and no one read them for themselves. I concluded that they weren't relevant for today. "Be good," I was told.

Well, I was a pretty good girl - most of the time, but my heart still wasn't at peace.

**Ocean Beach, New London, Connecticut 1954.**

My favorite summer pastime was a trip to the beach. A respite from the city's heat was nice. The sailors from the nearby Coast Guard station were even nicer! I had started modeling that spring and was very aware of the attention I could get. Marching up and down the boardwalk became a weekly ego trip. Flirting became a way of life.

On one of these excursions, I met a young sailor named Tony, and a summer romance began. There was only one insurmountable problem. Tony was an Italian Catholic, not a Jew. I was allowed to date only Jewish boys.

No problem! Tony had dark curly hair, brown eyes, and looked like the popular Jewish singer, Eddie Fisher. We'd change Tony's name to Mike Goldberg. My parents would never know.

So the deception began and continued through the summer. Fall came and school began. Beach days had ended with the first crisp, cool days of fall, and so did my infatuation with Tony. That is, until the day my mom confronted me. "Is Mike really Jewish?" she asked.

Defiantly, I answered, "No he isn't, and I don't care what he is. He's nice."

A rebellious heart, without knowledge of the offense it is to God, is a dangerous thing. Suddenly, the restriction made Tony more attractive than he had been all summer. Now I *had* to continue to see him.

Mom cried. She wept. She scolded. It was ridiculous to me. Why would a person's religion suddenly change his worth?

"Think of what people will say," she implored.

*Who cares,* I thought.

Years later, while reading the book of Deuteronomy, I read God's order to His chosen people concerning mixing with other peoples. *"...Thou shalt make no covenant with them, nor show mercy unto them. Neither shalt thou make marriages with them; thy daughter shalt thou not give to his son, nor his daughter shalt thou not take unto thy son. For they will turn away thy son from following me..."* (Deuteronomy 7:2b-4a).

What if I had been told that <u>God</u> cares?

By eighteen, my rebellion was full blown over the dating issue. Why wasn't there one Jewish man I was attracted to? Was it *forbidden fruit* that made Gentiles more attractive? I had vowed way back at the Tony incident never to hurt Mom again, so I met dates at the skating rink or at a movie theater. What she didn't see would never hurt her.

Little did I know that there was *Someone* watching my every move --*Someone* who neither slumbered nor slept.

Christmas continued through the years to bring a myriad of confusing thoughts to my mind. By Christmas 1957, I had a promising modeling career. The world was mine for the taking. *Why was I so empty inside?* I was away from home, yet I continued to hum when I heard THAT NAME in Christmas carols. *Who is that baby in the manger? What would happen to me if I said his name?* The questions plagued me, but I was afraid to find out.

Then I met Jim and my dating dilemma continued. Only this time things were different. For the first time in my life, I knew I was in love. It was only a matter of time before Jim wanted to meet my parents. With fear and trepidation, I made plans for a trip home. Not knowing how to prepare Jim for a negative reaction, I said nothing.

Jim almost immediately approached my parents with the question, "What would you think if I married your daughter?"

My mother frostily retorted, "Go marry one of your own kind."

Jim looked perplexed. I was human. He was human. What other kind was there?

Religion wasn't an issue for either of us. We dismissed it by agreeing that if we ever did marry, we'd find a religion that suited both of us.

Hurt and confused, I didn't want another "Tony scene." I was sick and tired of the hypocrisy of a religion practiced by the observance of a couple of holidays a year and rules I hated. The one I hated the most was, *You can't date non-Jews.* I considered this bigoted and unfair.

I wanted to turn to my dad, but that would have been futile. He was in the restaurant business, which allowed for a minimum of time at home during my waking hours. When he was there, he was very loving and very quiet. My mom was the dominant one - both in personality and presence. Dad had been raised in an orphanage from age five until he ran away to make it on his own at fourteen. Although Jewish by birth, his religious training was shallow, and religion was not a priority.

My mother, however, was raised in an Orthodox Jewish home, and religion was a way of life in her formative years. Any relationships with *Christians*, except in a superficial way, were unthinkable. After all, they were the ones who persecuted the Jews through the centuries, and the horrors of the holocaust were fresh in every Jewish mind in the 50's when I was a teenager. If you weren't a Jew, you were a *Christian*, was the predominant Jewish understanding, and *Christians* were to be kept at arm's length.

**Las Vegas, Nevada 1958**

My conflicting feelings of love for my parents and a deep desire to marry Jim stirred my rebellious heart into action. Jim left for Florida where his parents lived, and I bought a round-trip ticket to Las Vegas, Nevada. I wanted to get far away from everything and everyone I held dear. I needed time to think things over. Of course it was March and cold in the Northeast, so I chose a place where I could have fun - while I was thinking.

Stepping off the plane, I felt the warm spring breezes waft across the desert. The sun on my upturned face felt wonderful. Indeed, this would be the ideal place to rest, think, and have some fun at the same time.

"Where to?" the cab driver asked.

"Any nice hotel in the center of town," I replied.

In a few minutes I was registering in the Fremont Hotel - right in the heart of Las Vegas - in the midst of gambling casinos and nightclubs. The hotel was new and luxurious. I settled into my beautiful room and looked out the window. There on the opposite corner were the ever-flashing lights of the Golden Nugget casino calling to me. *Should*

*I go there first?* I wondered. Yawning, I decided that tomorrow would be soon enough. Taking a long bath and languishing in self-indulgence, I reflected on my plans - think a little, play a little, decide what to do about Jim.

Little did I realize that God had other plans for my life. He was about to answer those questions He had planted in my heart so many years before. *Who was the baby in the manger? What would happen if I said THAT NAME?*

As I went to bed that night, I noticed a Gideon Bible on the desk. *Maybe I'll read some of the New Testament,* I thought. *Maybe it'll give me some understanding of Jim's religion.* I had seen plenty of Bibles in hotel rooms as I traveled with my parents on vacation, but I never looked at one. I was told, "That's for *them.* " Whoever *them* was, it wasn't me, and I never touched one. This time was different. I was a long way from home and no one was there to check my curiosity.

Propping up on my fluffed pillows, I opened to the book of Matthew and began to read. *"The book of the generation of Jesus Christ, the son of David, the son of Abraham. Abraham begat Isaac; and Isaac begat Jacob; and Jacob begat..."* (Matthew I:1,2).

*Wait a minute! David, Abraham, Isaac and Jacob are <u>Jewish</u> patriarchs. Why are they mentioned with   THAT NAME?*

I  read through all the begats and finally came to verse 16, *"And Jacob begat Joseph the husband of Mary, of whom was born Jesus, who is called Christ."*

*This is talking about a Jewish baby!*

Continuing to read far into the night, I became absorbed in the amazing  story. The next day I continued to read, and the day after, and the day after that. I couldn't put the book down.

If anyone had told me that I'd never see Las Vegas when I was there, I would have thought him insane. After all, I came to have fun. I never saw a nightclub or a gambling casino. I was engrossed in a book I was forbidden to touch.

*"And Jesus, when he was baptized, went up straightway out of the water: and, lo, the heavens were opened unto him, and he saw the Spirit of God descending like a dove, and lighting upon him: And lo a*

*voice from heaven, saying, This is my beloved Son, in whom I am well pleased"* (Matthew 3:16,17).

*Is God  saying  that Jesus is his son?* I read on.

Chapters 5, 6, and 7 were a teaching on how to really live. The things Jesus taught became a balm to my selfish soul. If I could live by his teaching, I knew I'd find peace, yet everything this Jesus taught opposed my way of life. "Love your enemies?" I had enough trouble loving my friends!

The tenth chapter brought some real revelation. Jesus told his disciples, *"Go not into the way of the Gentiles, and into any city of the Samaritans enter ye not: But go rather to the lost sheep of the house of Israel"*  (Matthew 10:5,6).

*Jesus came to his own people, the Jews, not the Gentiles?* Why had I never heard this before?

Every page brought new conviction that Jesus was my Messiah, long awaited, yet missed by my people. *Maybe I can be a secret believer in Him,* I reasoned. Maybe my old philosophy of "what Mom doesn't know won't hurt her," was valid. Then I read, *"Whosoever therefore shall confess me before men, him will I confess also before my Father which is in heaven. But whosoever shall deny me before men, him will I also deny before my father which is in heaven"*  (Matthew 10:32,33).

*Guess I can't keep my decision to myself if I decide to follow Jesus.*

The next verses made me count the cost. *"Think not that I am come to send peace on earth: I came not to send peace, but a sword. For I am come to set a man at variance against his father, and the daughter against her mother, and the daughter-in-law against her mother-in-law. And a man's foes shall be they of his own household. He that loveth father or mother more than me is not worthy of me: and he that loveth son or daughter more than me is not worthy of me. And he that taketh not his cross, and followeth after me, is not worthy of me. He that findeth his life shall lose it: and he that loseth his life for my sake shall find it"* (Matthew 10:34-39). Was I willing to forsake, and be forsaken by a decision to believe in Jesus? It could mean being disowned by my family. *At least Jim would be happy,* I thought.

The more I read, the more light shone in the deep recesses of my being. I read through the Gospels. By the time I got to John, I was completely convinced. All the evidence was there, and questions that had been in my heart for so many years were being answered. *"The next day John seeth Jesus coming unto him, and saith, Behold the Lamb of God, which taketh away the sin of the world"* (John 1:29).

*Jesus was born in a stable! That's where lambs were supposed to be born! He became the sacrificial lamb by dying on a cross for the sins of the world. He was the fulfillment of the Passover lamb.*

*"For God so loved the world, that he gave his only begotten Son, that whosoever believeth in him shall not perish, but have everlasting life"* (John 3:16).

*"The Father loveth the Son and hath given all things into his hands. He that believeth not the Son shall not see life; but the wrath of God abideth on him"* (John 3:35,36).

Suddenly another thought became clear to me, *I wouldn't have to worry about an annual fast that never satisfied my questions about the sacrifice for sin. Jesus became the perfect, once and for all, sin offering. If I accept him, it's forever. I would have eternal life.*

Sitting trembling on the edge of the hotel bed, my heart felt as though it would pound out of my chest. An Old Testament verse took on new meaning. *"My mother and father may abandon me, but the Lord will take care of me"* I had decided to follow Jesus, no matter what the cost. What I didn't realize was that I was being born into a family far more vast, and infinitely more loving, than my natural family could ever be - the family of God.

In all my days of reading about Him, I still hadn't overcome the fear of saying THAT NAME. My childhood training was deep-rooted. How could I follow someone I couldn't call by his name? Taking a deep breath, I managed my first feeble prayer, "Jesus, I believe that you are my Messiah. Teach me to follow you."

I found out what would happen if I said THAT NAME. I was filled with such incredible joy and peace as He cleansed me and made me whole. I believed that the Bible was my new guidebook for life, and I truly became a new creature in Christ. Old things passed away, and all things became new **(II Corinthians 5:17)**. The joy I felt was beyond comprehension. The Bible talked about being "born again" when one accepts Jesus as their Savior, and I indeed felt brand new and clean. Now I wanted to tell someone. Jesus said to confess Him before men, and I didn't know any men in Las Vegas. *Jim!* I thought, *He'll be so happy!*

"Jim, guess what? I've been reading the Bible and discovered that Jesus is the Jewish Messiah. I decided to become a Christian!" I bubbled in excitement.

A long silence followed, and then the shocking, angry reply. "Why did you do that? We were going to find a religion that suited both of us."

Angry words were spoken, and the conversation ended. I had thought about rejection from my parents, but never from Jim. After all, wasn't he raised in a Christian family? Why wasn't he happy? But now, there was no turning back. I had counted the cost, and I had decided to follow Jesus - even if it meant losing Jim. Suddenly I realized that Jim knew **about** Jesus; he just didn't <u>know</u> Him.

My next phone call was to my parents. If the call to Jim was difficult, convincing my parents was impossible. It was apparent that I couldn't go home.

My boyfriend didn't want me, my parents didn't want me, but Jesus wanted me. That was all that mattered.

Tears of joy mingled with tears of grief. This was undoubtedly the happiest and saddest day of my life. By one decision, I found joy, peace and eternal life but lost my boyfriend and my family. I put aside the Bible and left the hotel. Wandering for blocks, I found myself standing in front of a beautiful Spanish style church. A sign marked PARSONAGE pointed to a house next door. I decided to knock on the door. "May I help you?" the kindly looking gentleman asked?

Blubbering, I replied, "I've just become a Christian and no one wants me."

Pastor Walter Bishop invited me into his home and called his wife. They patiently waited for me to regain my composure, and I told them my story. Ever so gently they encouraged me to trust Jesus, and they invited me to spend many happy hours with them that week. They prayed for me, they prayed for Jim and my parents, and they gave me some valuable guidelines in my future search for a church home.

That next Sunday was my first church experience. Mrs. Bishop encouraged me to confess Christ openly by walking to the front of the church at the end of the service. I wanted to, but I was so frightened! This dear lady took my hand and walked down the aisle with me. How indebted I am to the very first people to manifest the love of Christ. Before I left Las Vegas, the Bishops were sure to give me a New Testament of my own. Inscribed in the front were these words:

Dear SanDee,
You have been a real inspiration to all of us. Keep growing in your faith, study His Word and pray.
*"Let your light so shine before men, that they may see your good works, and glorify your Father which is in heaven"* (**Matthew 5:16**).

With our love and prayers,
The Bishops
March 28, 1958

That New Testament is one of my most treasured possessions.

Fortified by the Bishop's encouragement, I spent most of my remaining time in Las Vegas reading the rest of the New Testament. So many of the attitudes of my heart were dealt with as my mind was being renewed.

*"For he is not a Jew who is one outwardly; neither is that circumcision which is outward in the flesh; but he is a Jew who is one inwardly; and circumcision is that of the heart, in the spirit and not in the letter; whose praise is not of men, but God"* (**Romans 2:28,29**).

Suddenly there was a need to forgive those pretzel-eating, beer-drinking men on that Yom Kippur so long ago. *Forgive them Father; they didn't know <u>You.</u>*

So many truths were hidden in my heart in those lonely days in that hotel room. With no outside distractions, I grew in love and knowledge of my wonderful Jesus. He became not only my Savior but my Lord and my best friend.

Then one day the phone rang. It was a very sheepish Jim. "SanDee, I called to ask you to forgive me. For years, my mom has been praying for me. When I told her that I wanted to marry a Jewish girl, she threw up her hands in despair and told the Lord that she couldn't handle this. Apparently that was what God was waiting for. After our phone conversation last week, I told Mom that you had accepted Jesus and that I was angry. She told me in no uncertain terms what God would think if I discouraged you. I've thought a lot about it, and today I asked Jesus to be my Savior. Can you forgive me?"

Could I? I was only too happy to!

"I'd never be welcomed at home as a Christian," I told Jim. "I don't know what to do."

"Why don't you fly to Florida?" he replied, "My parents would like to meet you."

Trading my ticket to Connecticut for one to Miami, I flew south on April 2, 1958. The next Sunday would be my twentieth birthday and my first Easter as a Christian.

Jim greeted me at the plane, and our reunion had a special quality. No longer was Jim the most important person in my life, nor was I in his. Jesus had become the focus of our attention, and it was really good that He had. Our youthful impulsiveness would have headed us for disaster had it not been for God's protection.

As we got into the car to drive to Jim's home in West Palm Beach, he took my hand in his. Looking me straight in the eye, he said, "Since Sunday is Easter and your birthday, why not make it our wedding day? If we hurry, we can make it to the courthouse in time to get a license before they close."

Married? Why not? I never thought about the fact that Jim didn't have a job. Neither of us had much money. All my clothes and things were in Connecticut.

Another phone call to my poor parents. Little wonder they were less than pleased.

We made it to the courthouse in the nick of time, bought a license, and headed to Jim's parents' home. In my heart, I hoped it would take a long time to reach our destination. I was scared to death! *Will they welcome me or tell me to "go marry one of my own kind?"* I wondered.

My fears were relieved as soon as we walked in the door. Mom Stone met me with a big hug. I was going to be not only her daughter-in-law but also her sister in Christ - an answer to her prayers for Jim.

"Never in my wildest dreams did I expect God to answer my prayers for my son by a Jewish girl who found Christ in Las Vegas, Nevada!" she exclaimed.

We planned our wedding. It would be in a small church in the neighborhood. I would wear the blue and white embroidered sun dress I had with me. The white organdy coat that went with it would be perfect. I found a hat at a local store and attached some veiling to it. Jim's mom called their friends and family and baked a cake. For a few days everything was a blur of activity.

### April 6, 1958

The day had arrived. We attended church in the morning and returned that afternoon at three o'clock. The pastor was a stranger to me. I knew none of the guests except Jim's parents, sister, and two brothers whom I had met only three days before. Jim's long-time friend Paul was his best man. Carol, Paul's wife, was my matron of honor. I met her for the first time at the wedding rehearsal. I had never been to a church wedding before my own.

When it came to the part in the ceremony for me to place the ring on Jim's finger, he kept pulling his hand back.

*Oh, no,* I thought, *He doesn't want to marry me.*

Close to tears, I finally got the message. I was so nervous that I was trying to shove the ring on the wrong hand!

If only Mom and Dad could have been there. I was so happy, yet my joy was tinged with sadness at their absence. It took time and patient love to restore a relationship with them.

Had I returned to Connecticut, this may never have happened. Orthodox Jewish tradition requires an actual funeral for a child who converts to Christianity. The pressure from family and the Jewish community might have persuaded my parents to do this. By my living so far away, it was easier to save face. Before long, they visited us in Florida. I was their child, and they loved me in spite of my choices.

The day came when I'm sure they realized that my faith in Jesus Christ had changed me for the better. The peace and joy I was experiencing had to show in the letters I wrote, along with my deepening sense of responsibility to honor God by honoring my parents. Our first child, their first grandchild, brought about a great healing.

## Chapter Two

## Acknowledging Him as Parenthood Planner

*"Lo children are an heritage from the Lord, and the fruit of the womb is his reward. "* (Psalm 127:3)

My heart pounded as I waited in the obstetrician's office for the results of the test. Was I pregnant or not?

"SanDee Stone," the nurse called out. She ushered me into the doctor's office. After greeting me, Dr. Jackson invited me to sit down as he discussed the results of his examination and the pregnancy test. He gently explained, "Your ovaries are full of cysts, preventing you from conceiving. It would be best to schedule a hysterectomy."

Incredulously, I asked, "I'm not pregnant?" That was why I thought I had come to see him.

"No," he replied, "You were late because of the formation of the cysts. If you ever conceived, it could be very dangerous to your health. I'm really sorry, but a hysterectomy as soon as possible would be best."

The appointment was made to enter the hospital in a few days. How could Dr. Jackson possibly know that his diagnosis was shattering a lifelong dream? Some girls dream of a trip to far away places, or of a career, or of a fancy home and rich husband. Growing up, I dreamt about children. From age eleven I baby-sat; and as I cuddled other people's babies, I thought about the day I'd have my own. My dream was to marry and have four children - two boys and two girls. Now, in a few harsh, clinical moments, that dream was dispelled like so much air.

Driving home, I cried. Oh, how I cried! I was twenty years old and had been so happy this last month, thinking a baby was on the way.

Jim tried to comfort me. "We can adopt a baby, honey." I couldn't be comforted. I wanted to bear a baby of my own.

Sleep was slow in coming that night. I thought my heart would break. As I lay in bed listening to Jim's even breathing next to me, a Scripture verse crept into my troubled mind. *"Jesus Christ, the same yesterday, and today, and forever. "* (Hebrews 13:8). If that were true, and I knew it was, He could heal me just as He healed when He was here on earth. After all, didn't the verse say that He never changes? Faith began to grow in my heart as I lay there meditating on His Word.

*Jesus,* I began to pray silently, *I don't want to ask you for one baby. In Psalm 37, you said you'd give the desire of my heart if I delighted in you. I do delight in you, Lord. Please let me have four children - four normal and healthy children - two boys and two girls. In Jesus' name, Amen.*

I drifted off into a deep and peaceful sleep, knowing that my prayer had been heard and would be answered, in His time.

Waking the next morning, I found Jim already up and tiptoeing around the room as he dressed for work. I greeted my concerned husband with a big grin and a cheerful, "Hi, honey, Good morning." After my inconsolable tears the night before, he looked at me in astonishment. "What's happened to you?" he asked.

Quite confidently, I informed him, "We're going to have four children - two boys and two girls. I'm going to cancel the surgery." Bouncing out of bed, I went on to explain what had happened the night before. If Jim thought I had lost my mind, he was tactful enough not to comment. Whether or not he shared my faith at that moment, he certainly preferred a radiant wife to a tearful one.

I couldn't wait for Doctor Jackson's office to open that morning. Precisely at nine o'clock I called and asked to speak to him. He was with a patient, so I waited for him to return my call. Every second that clicked by was agony. I was so eager to share my good news. Finally the phone rang, and the doctor was on the other end. Not one to beat around the bush, I plunged right in. "Dr. Jackson, please cancel the surgery I'm scheduled for. I've prayed, and I'm going to have four children - two boys and two girls."

"Mrs. Stone, when can you come in to my office," he replied. That was it. I naively thought he'd be as overjoyed as I was.

Later that day, I again sat across the desk from a concerned looking doctor. He again explained my present condition and the danger to my health if I refused surgery. Patiently, I told him about my prayer session the night before, the scriptures that God had spoken to my heart, and that I would bear four children. With a woeful expression on his face, he ended the visit. I'm sure he thought I needed a psychiatrist, not an obstetrician.

Three months later, the county fair opened. I had never been to a fair and persuaded Jim to take me. I enjoyed looking at the various displays of canned fruits and vegetables, sewing projects, and the farm animals, but most of all I loved the midway. Being more kid than adult, I coaxed Jim to take me on all the rides. I loved the ferris wheel, the octopus, and the roller coaster. After a few rides though, my stomach was churning, and the cotton candy I had just enjoyed wasn't sitting so well. "Ooh, I'm so sick," I complained to Jim. "Maybe I'm getting old. Rides never bothered me before. Can we go home?"

"Maybe you're pregnant!" he joked.

It was no joke! I *was* pregnant. Returning to Dr. Jackson's office, he confirmed that our first baby was on the way and cautioned that I'd have to be closely monitored. I was jubilant! Here was the beginning of my first real answer to prayer. "This is number one of four," I told everyone who would listen. "God promised me."

In the beginning, even a case of morning, noon, and night sickness couldn't dampen my happiness at being pregnant. Fighting nausea I valiantly cooked dinner each night. Greeting Jim at the door when he returned from work with a "Hi, honey," I would head for the bathroom!

The sickness passed with the first trimester, and I loved being pregnant. I made and wore maternity clothes long before I needed to, as an announcement to the world of my joy. As I felt the first stirrings of that little life within me, I continually praised God for His goodness to me. I somehow looked at this baby as His blessing and confirmation of our marriage.

My due date was set for September 8, 1959. I busied myself in preparing the nursery. On one whole wall, I painted a circus scene. By September, a baby shower had been given to me by the ladies of our church. The crib was set up, dresser filled, and myriads of baby equipment ready. All we needed was a baby.

Our little house had no air conditioning, and I was getting very uncomfortable. The days began to drag. My due date came and went, and I definitely was not a happy camper!

I had never thought about something going wrong until a well meaning elderly lady asked when I was due. "Ten days ago," I lamented.

"Well!" she began, "I have a sister whose first baby was late, and the baby was dead."

I didn't need to hear that and had to spend some time in prayer to overcome the overwhelming fear I had felt as she spoke. Soon my peace was restored, and I remembered my prayer for normal, healthy babies. I wondered how anyone could be so insensitive.

Jim and I were living next door to his parents. Jim's brother Ken and his wife, Mae, lived next door to Mom and Dad on the other side. Mae was expecting a baby a short time after me. If sibling rivalry is a reality, so is sister-in-law rivalry. I was due first and was determined to have my baby before Mae. God had a way of dealing with my selfish attitude. On September 20, Mae went into labor and gave birth to a baby girl, Debbie. I mustered up all the forgiveness I could that Sunday afternoon, and Jim and I went to the hospital to visit Mae. I truly rejoiced with her, yet ached to hold my own baby. Looking at all the little ones in the hospital nursery was sheer torture. A nurse came into Mae's room to inform her roommate that she was being released the next morning, and I impulsively said to her, "Save the bed for me. I'm coming in."

That evening we had dinner at Mom and Dad Stone's house. I remember sitting on Jim's lap in Dad's big blue recliner and crying in frustration. I was so tired of waiting!

### September 21, 1959

At five o'clock in the morning, my water broke and labor began with full intensity. I thrilled with each contraction, knowing that our long-awaited baby would soon be here. On the way to the hospital, the foremost thought in my mind was to warn Jim, "Don't tell Mae; I want to surprise her!"

"Please let me be awake," I pleaded with Dr. Jackson. In those days, it was customary to be put to sleep, but I wanted to experience every moment of childbirth.

Husbands weren't allowed in the labor or delivery room, so Jim was ushered into a waiting room as I was being prepped for delivery. When I kissed him good-bye, I was far more worried about him than me. His face was ashen and his stomach was upset. Frequently I'd ask the nurse to check on him. Quite a switch!

At 9:00 a.m., I was wheeled into the delivery room. It was almost over! Propped up on my elbows so that I could see in a mirror, I beheld a miracle. An eight pound, six ounce baby girl quietly pushed her way into the world. No complications. Loryn Elise, our precious gift from God, had a head full of dark ringlets, and I was sure she was the most beautiful baby ever born.

We appreciated the significance of her names: Loryn - a laurel, symbol of victory; Elise - consecrated to God. Having her **was** a victory, and what a joy to know we would raise her to love and serve our Lord. We dedicated her back to Him for His guidance and care.

Soon I was wheeled from the recovery room to the bed next to Mae, just as I had predicted the day before! Those few days in the hospital together were so much fun. We especially giggled every time our babies were brought to us. The nurses would unwrap each baby and check their name bracelets on their ankles - as if we didn't know our own babies!

When Loryn had just passed her first birthday, I again felt those telltale symptoms I had felt at the fair. Only this time, there were no rides to upset my stomach. Baby number two was on the way!

After Loryn's birth, Dr. Jackson emphasized how lucky I had been to have had a normal, healthy pregnancy and delivery. He assured me that it probably wouldn't happen again. "It wasn't luck," I told him, "God answered prayer. There are three more children to come. You'll see!"

Now I was pregnant again. Half of my prayer for four children would be complete.

Then something happened for which I was totally unprepared. My dad had major surgery on his leg in February, and the large cast from hip to ankle made moving around cumbersome. Since Florida was an easier place to recuperate, my parents were staying with us. Both of my parents were enjoying time with Loryn, their pride and joy, and I was enjoying our restored relationship with them. I still couldn't talk about Jesus, but I could manifest His love through my actions.

One rainy, sleepy afternoon, Loryn was taking a nap in her nursery in the front of our wood frame house, and Dad was asleep in the back bedroom. I decided that a cup of coffee would just hit the spot, so I put the kettle on the stove to boil water.

All of a sudden, flames shot up from the burner. Panicking, all my mind could grasp was that the baby was in the front of the house, and Dad was in the back, both asleep. How could I get them out? What I didn't realize was that the electric coil on the stove had shorted out and burned a hole in the kettle. The water quickly extinguished the flames.

The intense shock took its toll on my system. By the next morning, I began to have severe contractions. That evening, I miscarried the baby. Lying there in the hospital in the quiet of the night, I cried out to the Lord. *Why did I lose this baby when I wanted it so much.?*

As I reached beyond the hurt and disappointment, I knew two things: God had everything in control, and my reaction in front of my parents would be important. I had asked the Lord for four normal, healthy children, and I felt assured in my heart that my prayer was still to be answered in its entirety. The realization that we'd someday see this baby that we lost brought me peace. I could grieve, yet not as those who have no hope. Heaven would make our separated family complete.

Within a month, I discovered that I was pregnant again. *Oh, thank you Lord,* my grateful heart cried. This pregnancy was to be as normal as Loryn's had been.

### Jupiter, Florida June 1961

With the first hint of spring in Connecticut, my parents returned home. We were busy preparing for a move of our own to Jupiter, a small town about thirty miles north of West Palm Beach. Living there would allow Jim less travel time to his job in the computing lab at Pratt and Whitney Aircraft. The house we were having built in a new sub-division was complete, and we busied ourselves with packing, moving, and settling in. Our home would have three bedrooms and two baths - much needed extra space for our expanding family.

## December 14, 1961

A few days less than nine months after my miscarriage, we were on our way to the hospital again. Half an hour after arriving, eight pound, twelve ounce Timothy David was born. His name means honoring God, beloved. A special name for a special answer to prayer. Our dark-haired, dark-eyed son was surely the second most beautiful baby I'd ever seen! Loryn loved to "help" Mommy with baby brother. We continually rejoiced in God's goodness to us.

## July 4, 1963

As I looked out the hospital window at the darkening sky, a burst of red, white, and blue rockets exploded up above. The fireworks were celebrating the birth of our nation, but to me, they seemed to celebrate the birth of seven pound Jeffrey Todd, born that afternoon. This little guy had blond hair and blue eyes - I was glad I was awake at his birth, or I might have thought they switched babies!

Jeffrey - Divinely peaceful. *May you always live up to the meaning of your name!*

*Three precious children to raise for you, Lord. How I praise you.* The answer to my prayer was three-quarters complete.

It was hard to ever convince Jeff that all the fireworks on the Fourth of July weren't his special birthday celebration!

## August 21, 1965

The day I went into labor with our fourth child was momentous in world history - the day of the first manned space flight. Yet that occasion paled in significance when I compared it to the event taking place in the delivery room at Good Samaritan Hospital that day. My faithful doctor, who had witnessed three miracles, was with me to witness the fourth. Just as the baby was about to be born, Dr. Jackson quipped, "This is going to be a nice, big boy!"

I looked up at him, gasping through the last hard contractions and replied, "Dr. Jackson! You've seen God answer my prayer three-quarters of the way. You know this has to be a girl!"

In a few minutes, eight pound Bonnie Allison made her entrance into the world. What a beautiful sight to see our tiny baby girl in the arms of that big doctor, as tears filled his eyes. Dr. Jackson had experienced with us the power of God and answered prayer.

From the time I was pregnant with Tim, Loryn eagerly anticipated a baby sister she named Bonnie. She never forgot! Bonnie - sweet and good - a fitting completion to our family.

It seems that God uses people in my life to redirect my thoughts to his specific promises to me. When our children were very young, a lady approached me in the grocery store and admired the behavior of the children. She casually asked their ages. "One, three, four and a half, and six," I replied.

Her next remark was, "Wow, you'll have four rebellious teenagers at the same time!"

"No I won't," I retorted. "These children are all an answer to prayer and are dedicated to God. They are His, and they will be trained to love and serve Him."

That confrontation was to replay in my mind many times through the child-rearing years, when I reminded the children (and Satan) that they belonged to God. No matter what the outward circumstances were, I would never give the Devil a foothold in any of my children's lives.

To insure our part in protecting them, Jim and I took seriously the admonitions in scripture concerning the training of our children. Jim had a strong conviction that training them was his responsibility, not the Sunday school teacher's or the pastor's. *"Train up a child in the way he should go ....,"* Jim quoted to me from **Proverbs 22:6.** Every night, we had family altar. Jim played his guitar, led the children in choruses they loved, and read scripture to them. How many times I have thanked God for a husband with the strength to live out his convictions in our family.

For us to take the responsibility that God commanded was work. It required prayer that we would make the right decisions in guiding each child. It took disciplining them according to scripture. Most of all, it took guarding our own lives so that we could be devoid of hypocrisy.

When the children were very young, Jim and I made a covenant with God. We pledged not to read anything we wouldn't allow our children to read. We agreed not to indulge in a habit we didn't want our children to have. We chose not to go anywhere that we couldn't freely take them. Was it worth the sacrifice? We can assuredly say, "Yes!" Doing things God's way always is. All four children accepted Christ at a young age, and as adults, are married to Christian mates. They are actively serving Jesus together.

After Bonnie was born, we were sure our family was complete. God had given me the desire of my heart - four children - two boys and two girls. But God is full of surprises! When we committed our ways to his keeping, believing that we could trust Him to direct our paths, many circumstances we hadn't planned came into our lives. Jim told me, "When we are saved, God has us sign a blank contract and He fills it in as we go along. We couldn't handle knowing everything in advance."

When Bonnie was fourteen, another baby was on the way - this time with no morning sickness! We were living in New York. Our daughter Loryn was working as a counselor for the Walter Hoving Home, a Christian drug and alcohol program. An unwed mother had come into the program to seek freedom from her drug addiction, and she needed someone to care for her infant son who would be one year old on February 2.

Bonnie had always prayed for a baby brother and that desire was the conclusion of her every Christmas list. Loryn had a wonderful idea! Here was a baby who needed a home for nine months, and Bonnie needed a baby brother - at least for a while! She called us with this brainstorm, and we said we'd pray about it. God said, "Yes!"

**February 3, 1980**

A pickup truck drove up to our yard, and a counselor couple from the program stood at the door with a little blond-haired, green-eyed baby in tow. They unpacked the little bit of clothing he possessed, a crib, and a high chair; then they left.

Bonnie was ecstatic! I was wondering, *What in the world have we done! I'm forty-one years old and haven't had a baby around in a long time. Besides, this little boy looks so lost and sad. Can we ever meet his needs?*

Joshua Thomas settled into our routine and into our hearts. Bonnie assumed responsibility for much of his care when she wasn't in school and loved every minute. I, surprisingly, adjusted to having a baby in the house.

About that time, God had another big surprise for us - another child was on the way! This was really a BIG surprise, as Richard Timothy was sixteen years old.

A social worker with whom Jim was acquainted approached him with a question. "Would you be interested in having a boy who needs to be moved from his present foster home live with your family?" she asked. Betty knew we occasionally opened our home to people who needed a temporary place to stay. "Richard recently became a Christian." she added. We were surprised to learn that the boy she was talking about was already a casual school friend of our son Jeff.

That night we held a family conference. Our policy was never to welcome anyone into our home to stay unless every family member was in agreement. We felt that policy would insure that our children were part of the solution, not part of the problem. It was unanimously decided that we all wanted Rich to come.

The next meeting was held with Rich. There were some stipulations to living in our home. He would have to decide if he even wanted to live with us. Jim outlined the general rules of conduct we had for our children. Then he told Rich, "We are not a licensed foster home, and we choose not to be. If you come to live with us, we will welcome you as one of the family, with all the restrictions and benefits our own children have. It would mean leaving the state foster care program and all the financial benefits that you have been accustomed to having - clothing, medical and dental care, and your future college education. In a nutshell, it would mean trusting the Lord, instead of the state of New

York, to meet your needs." During the next week, Rich severed his ties with the foster care program and moved into our home, and into our hearts, too.

The nine months we were to keep Joshua sped by all too quickly. He had gone from a forlorn little guy to a delightfully happy baby.

In December, Joshua's birth-mother was to leave the Walter Hoving Home. We invited her to live with us for a while as she reestablished her relationship with her son. After a few weeks, it became apparent that she had decided not to live a Christian life, and we feared for Joshua's future. We loved him so much by then, and our desire was to see him raised in a Christian home. Lana would have a hard enough time being a single mom, even with the Lord to help her. Without Him, we felt it would be impossible. We had a conference with Lana and encouraged her to choose righteousness for Joshua's sake. She had heard the truth of Jesus Christ every day for the past nine months, yet without repentance.

"I never even wanted a baby," she tearfully blurted out. "I had two abortions before and don't know why I didn't abort this one. I'd like to be his sister, not his mother."

Yet, without even understanding the implications, Lana had named him Joshua. The name means, "God saves."

Our recommendation to Lana was that she return to her home state, many miles away. We suggested that she take six months to decide what she was going to do with Joshua. Not wanting her to make an emotional decision, we also proposed that she not visit our home during that time.

At the end of the six months, Lana knew that she was not ready to commit to being a mother or to follow Jesus. She was unselfish enough to want a better life for Joshua. "My parents were divorced when I was five years old," she said. "I grew up without my dad, in a non-Christian environment. If you'll adopt him, I'll release him to you." Our minds were in a turmoil. There were so many questions. *Was it fair to Joshua to have "old" parents? Would he always regret not having little brothers or sisters to play with?* Most of all we wondered, *What is God's will?* We didn't want to make an emotional decision either.

Interestingly, it was Richard whom God used to help us decide.

"Don't let happen to him what happened to me," he cried imploringly. "It's too late for me."

What had happened to Rich was sad. When he was two years old, his parents divorced. Neither one wanted their child, and he became a ward of the state, spending fourteen years in foster homes. He was never released for adoption.

"What do you mean it's too late?" I replied. "Nothing is ever too late for God."

"You mean that I can be adopted?" Rich asked. "Would you adopt me?" Now he was nearing eighteen years old, when he could make that decision for himself.

**Courthouse, Ulster County, New York  December 10, 1981**

What a wonderful blessing was in store for us when we decided to let God plan our family. Richard and Joshua became our sons on the same day. A friend shared this poem with me, and it reflects all that is in my heart toward these two special boys.

### Child of My Heart

. . . I could not love you any more,
Or any less.

## Chapter Three

## Acknowledging Him as Healer

*".....I am the Lord that healeth thee."*    Exodus 15:26b

**West Palm Beach, Florida Summer 1970**

Eagles are interesting birds. The mother eagle prepares for her young by building a nest on the protected craggy heights of a cliff. She prepares a wonderfully comfortable bed of soft down and then lays her eggs. Finally, the little eaglets hatch and are sheltered by the warmth of the soft down and their mother's warm body covering them, shielding them from the harsh elements high on the cliff. She leaves only long enough to forage for food for her open-mouthed, voraciously hungry babies.

The day comes though when it's time for the eaglets to leave the nest and learn to fly on their own. They are very reluctant; after all, they have had all their creature comforts met by Mom!

Well, Mom has other ideas. Suddenly, she begins to pick up the soft down in her strong beak and toss it over the edge of the nest. The feathers disappear in the wind, and the eaglets are very uncomfortable. Where there was once soft cushioning, they find stiff, harsh twigs poking their tender bodies. The Bible describes this when it speaks of the eagle "stirring up" its nest **(Deuteronomy 32:11).**

Then mother eagle does a terrible thing! One by one, she shoves her terrified babies over the edge of the nest. As they hurtle rapidly to the rocks below, they flap and squawk frantically. Before reaching the bottom, however, their mother swoops down under each one, places them on her back, and with her strong wings carries them back to the nest.

Day after day, this process is repeated as the baby's wings are being exercised and strengthened. The day finally comes when they're strong enough to have the faith to fly on their own.

Sometimes God must allow us to be shaken out of our comfortable nest so that we can "learn to fly" in our walk of faith. We can't remain babies forever, nestled in the soft down of an easy life.

Strength, we soon learn, comes through adversity. The purpose isn't to harm us but to draw us closer in trusting God.

In May, 1970, my comfortable nest, and that of my family, was "stirred" up! Apprehensively, once again I sat in Dr. Jackson's office, following his examination for the cause of a persistent pain in my right breast. He had examined me before, when I had complained about the pain, but found nothing. I felt a little foolish calling him again; but had I noticed a small dark spot that looked like dried blood in my bra, as I undressed for bed the night before. I remembered articles in the Reader's Digest with the list of the warning signs of cancer, and I thought I'd better call the doctor. ANY UNNATURAL BLEEDING was on the list. I hoped he'd tell me to stop worrying. Instead, he told me to come right into his office.

Breathlessly, I waited for his response to the examination. His face broke out in a big grin as he said, "There's nothing to worry about. You have a polyp on a milk gland in your breast, and they're never malignant. I'm going to send you to a surgeon, however, because he may suggest removing the polyp. That would also remove the discomfort you're feeling. Before I do though," he continued, "I want you to know that Dr. Robins is somewhat of a pessimist. He'll probably prepare you for the worst, but don't let that alarm you. He just likes to be able to tell his patients, *It was nothing serious,* when the surgery is over."

Leaving Dr. Jackson, I drove to Dr. Robins' office in the next block. He had agreed to see me immediately. On the way there, I pondered my predicament. I was freshly reminded of a remark I had made to Jim a few months before. "If that ever happened to me," I cried, "I'd rather be dead!" A lady I sewed for had had a radical mastectomy, and it really shook me. I feared physical deformity of any kind.

My mind was so relieved after the positive visit with Dr. Jackson. *Could I handle Dr. Robins' pessimism?* I wondered.

My apprehension gave way to giddy relief as I sat across the desk from Dr. Robins. He showed me a magazine, the page turned to a pizza ad. In full color was a picture of a pizza, cut in slices, with an olive in the center. "Picture this pizza as a breast," he began. " You do have a  polyp on a milk gland. The procedure is simple. I would remove the slice of your breast that includes the polyp and sew the other sections adjoining that one together. You'd be in the hospital overnight. I've never seen a malignant polyp in a breast. You can have it removed next week, or wait if you wish."

My mind was immediately at peace. If that was the report of a pessimist, this would be a breeze!

Jim and I decided to schedule the surgery for the following week. A friend was able to take care of the four children for a day or two, and summer vacation had begun.

Confidently, I checked into Good Samaritan Hospital. Jim had suggested the luxury of a private room for the one night I'd be there, a mini-vacation from the rigors of homemaking. Meals in bed, remote control TV, and a window facing beautiful Lake Worth - I could handle this!

Visiting hours were over, and Jim left me alone. I settled into bed for the night and opened my Bible. *Lord, give me a verse to hold on to,* I prayed.

My eyes fell on the page where my Bible opened, and I read: *"And he said unto me, My grace is sufficient for thee: for my strength is made perfect in weakness. Most gladly therefore will I rather glory in my infirmities, that the power of Christ may rest upon me. Therefore I take pleasure in infirmities, in reproaches, in necessities, in persecutions, in distresses for Christ's sake: for when I am weak, then am I strong. "* (II Corinthians 12:9,10). *That's nice,* I thought, *His strength would be perfected in my weakness.* I fell into a deep and peaceful sleep.

I was wheeled into the operating room the next morning. The anesthetic quickly took effect, and the next memory I had was of waking up in the recovery room. My chest felt as though a ton of bricks was pressing down on it. In the hazy fog of awakening, I focused on an IV bag strung on a pole next to me and a tube tied to my left hand. The substance in the bag looked red, like blood. *A blood transfusion,* I thought. Flooding into my mind came the chilling realization, *It WAS cancer. My breast is gone!*

Accompanying the thought was the most overwhelming flood of the deepest, most joyful peace I had ever experienced. It was one thing to know intellectually that the Bible promises a peace that passes all understanding; it was another thing to experience it.

When I awoke the next time, I was in my own hospital room. Jim was hovering over me, deep concern etched on his tense and anguished face. The ton of bricks was still on my chest, and I asked, "Was everything all right?" I don't know why I asked, because I already knew the answer.

"No, honey," he replied, patting my hand in despair. "They had to take your breast."

"It's okay," I replied. "I have so much peace."

Drifting off to sleep again, the scene had changed by the next time I awoke. Instead of a worried looking husband standing there, I focused on a worried looking doctor.

"Don't be concerned about telling me, Dr. Robins. I already know that you removed my breast, and I'm okay." The peace persisted. When I remembered my anguish a few months earlier over a lady I hardly knew, I was sure, beyond a doubt, of the supernatural peace only the Lord could give to me.

The next morning I awoke early, read my Bible, brushed my hair, and began a letter to a friend. Except for the feeling of a heavy weight on my chest, I had no pain. The shocked doctor walked into my room at 9:00 a.m. and asked, "Who fixed your hair?"

"I did," I replied. No one had told me that I should expect limited use of my arm.

My overnight stay in the hospital extended to ten days. What a value Christian friends were during that time. Ginny, who had agreed to keep the children overnight, didn't even flinch. "Relax," she encouraged me. "They are doing fine. I'll keep them as long as you need me to."

Every day, sad looking friends paraded into my room. They were at a loss for words. I was thirty-two years old and had cancer. What *can* you say? I tried to make them feel more at ease. I was doing fine.

Jim looked awful. A close friend quipped, "Jim should be in the hospital instead of you. You look great, and he looks terrible!"

Little did I realize the shocking prognosis that would accompany the return of the tests performed on the lymph nodes that had been removed. The cancer had spread to my lymph system. Medically and statistically, there was no hope. Nothing, even this news, could shake my peace. Not even Dr. Robins, who feared that I wasn't facing reality. "Don't you know how serious your condition is? Don't you know you're going to die?" he implored.

Of course I knew, yet I knew something  that he, as a nonbeliever, couldn't possibly know. I knew that I COULDN'T LOSE! If I died, I'd go to heaven. After all, wasn't I told in the Bible that *"To be absent from the body is to be present with the Lord?"* What more could I ask? Didn't Paul teach that to die (for a Christian) is gain?

Never was my faith in Jesus Christ more precious, or the hope of heaven more real. As the days went by, Dr. Robins tried every way he could to help me "face reality." He was sure my lack of tears was a defense mechanism that would crumble in the trying days ahead.

One day during a visit for a regular checkup, I tried as clearly as I could to share my faith with Dr. Robins. He had just asked if I minded losing my breast. I was lying on the examining table feeling very vulnerable. The surgery was terribly disfiguring, but the Lord truly was helping me cope. "Dr. Robins," I began, "if I die, I'm going to heaven, and there my body will be whole. If I live, I'll live for Jesus Christ. My body is just the house my soul lives in. With or without a breast, I want my life to glorify Him."

*Was this really scaredy-cat me?* No, this was God's grace to help in time of need.

That was the last time I ever saw Dr. Robins. In the next few days, we received a registered letter from him. It said that I would need further medical treatment in the days ahead, and he would like me to find another doctor who could help me face the seriousness of my condition. He went on to say that he would accept the insurance payment, and we could forget the balance of his bill.

I had never cried over my own condition, but after reading that letter, I wept over Dr. Robins'. He had come face to face with the reality of Jesus Christ and had turned away.

Dr. Jackson was another story. He sat on a chair in my hospital room the day after surgery and cried. He felt responsible for not discovering the problem earlier. I tried to console him with the reassurance that my life was in God's hands. Dr. Jackson's gratitude was rewarding. After all, had he not seen God intervene in my life when the children were born?

A month after the mastectomy, Dr. Jackson suggested that I have a hysterectomy. "It won't cure the cancer," he cautioned, "but it will get rid of the estrogen in your body that may cause it to grow faster. We possibly can give you a few good months." Back to the hospital, I went. Back to Ginny's house trooped the kids.

On being released from the hospital, Dr. Jackson wrote a prescription for tranquilizers. They would ward off the effects of a total hysterectomy at such a young age. I could expect sleepless nights, hot flashes, and periods of depression, I was warned.

I never filled the prescription. I was thrown back to the faith I had in that hotel room in Las Vegas and to the faith I had when I implored God for my four children. In the world's eyes, my situation was hopeless. *Hopeless!* I thought. *I think God likes that word! When we reach the end of our own strength, His strength is perfected.* I had read that in the hospital the night before surgery. It was becoming truth to my spirit.

I basked in the warmth of Jesus' love in those days. Flat on my back, I had time to look up to Him. The everyday cares of a normal household with young children had left me little time in the past to attend to my own spiritual needs. Now I had abundant time and appreciated it immensely.

Friends from church took over my housework, care of the children, and every evening someone was at the door with a hot meal before Jim returned from work. At this time, my sisters in Christ didn't ask what they could do; they just did it.

One of the things I loved to do was read. Yet, because I had so little time to indulge in books, I resorted to quick stories in women's magazines. Now a whole new world of reading was opening up to me. Many visitors gave me books as "get-well" gifts. They were a balm to my soul. The Christian's Secret of a Happy Life, by Hannah Whitall Smith; Realities, by Mother Basilea Schlink; Sit, Walk, and Stand, by Watchman Nee; and I Believe in Miracles, by Kathryn Kuhlman, became my most treasured companions. These books helped me to realize that whether I lived another day or many more years, Jesus had to be central in my life. Everything I did had to focus on Him.

I meditated on our life as a whole. Jim was building a career in data processing with RCA Corporation. The children required a large block of our time. Oh, we still had devotions almost every day and went to church each week, but without even realizing it, we had placed Jesus on the sidelines of our life. No longer was He in the center.

Facing the reality of how little time I had left, I was brought to a crisis decision.The Word of God began to live in my heart in a new way. "If you love me, keep my commandments," Jesus had said. I realized that my goals and my plans were of no consequence. Suddenly my focus changed from what Jesus could do for me, to what I could do for Him. What could I do in response to the love that sent Him to the cross for me?

Reading the Bible one day, I was convicted of the time I had spent reading secular magazines and watching TV. *"Finally, brethren, whatsoever things are true, whatsoever things are honest, whatsoever things are pure, whatsoever things are lovely, whatsoever things are of good report; if there be any virtue, and if there be any praise, think on these things"* (Philippians 4:8). Out went my magazines; off went the TV. If I had time to spare in the future, I would fill it by thinking about good things that would glorify Him.

These days of recuperation were blessed - filled with love and concern from Jim, the children, and friends. I felt surrounded by a bubble of protection.

Jim was living his own personal encounter with God during these months. I've asked him to share from his perspective.

**Jim's Story**

It's difficult to describe my feelings when I learned of SanDee's cancer. The shock was heightened by the contrast of my overconfidence that nothing was really wrong with her. She was going to be in the hospital overnight - a minor inconvenience, that was all.

To occupy my time while sitting in the waiting room, I leafed through the pile of magazines on the table. *It's taking longer than I expected,* I thought. Getting up to stretch my legs, I went in search of more magazines. More time passed. The intercom finally droned, "Mr. Stone, Mr. Jim Stone, ...please report to third-floor surgery."

The intensity of my confidence never let the thought occur to me that something might be wrong. I was mildly puzzled all the way to the third floor anteroom.

A doctor with a surgical mask over his mouth greeted me. "Mr. Stone?"

"Yes, what's up?" I asked.

"I have bad news, Mr. Stone," he replied. "We routinely sent samples to the lab for examination, and I'm afraid that your wife has a malignancy in her breast. I need your permission to perform a radical mastectomy. I'll do all I can to help her."

I'm sure I was in shock, for I nonchalantly signed the form. Dr. Robins returned to the operating room, and I stood staring after him down the hallway. The doors through which he disappeared said: AUTHORIZED PERSONNEL ONLY BEYOND THIS POINT. Maybe it was then that reality hit me. *SanDee has CANCER! That which I feared most has come upon me,* I thought.

Dr. Robins had suggested that I go home for a while, since the surgery and time in the recovery room would be several hours. Stumbling blindly through my tears, I made my way down to the first floor and out into the parking lot. Dazed is the best description of how I felt.

*Oh, God,* I prayed. *You are the only hope I have. The best surgeon in the Palm Beach area just told me that he could do nothing more to help SanDee. He said that no hospital in the country has better equipment than Good Samaritan. God, you are truly my only hope.*

A still, small voice somehow forced its way into the screaming plea within my mind. *Faith cometh by hearing, and hearing by the Word of God.* That phrase was to echo in my brain many more times on the way home. It became a strange source of comfort to me.

When I returned home, I opened a New Testament and began to read. Each time a case of healing was mentioned, I underlined it with a bright red pencil. *I'm going to underline these, then reread them until the Word of God has built my faith,* I vowed.

Later that evening, I visited SanDee. I unsuccessfully tried to hide the anguish I felt in my heart, although I was somewhat comforted by the peace she seemed to have.

The next day I had a conference with the surgeon. "What are SanDee's chances for survival?" I asked.

"We'll have to wait for the final report on the lymph nodes which were sent to the lab. If they're clean, she will statistically have, perhaps, an eighty percent chance of non-recurrence. The more nodes affected, the more the statistical chances drop. This would indicate the fact that the cancer has spread," he replied.

I continued to beseech God and underline in the Bible. When I had almost completed the book of John, something within me said, *Jesus was the Son of God. What do you hope to accomplish by reading about HIS success?*

That discouraged me (which was Satan's intent) until I decided to go on into the book of Acts. After reading several accounts of healing, I thought about my training on dispensations. I had been taught that God deals with man differently, depending on the era or "dispensation." *Since Jesus has ascended and not yet returned,* I reasoned, *this places Peter and me in the same dispensation. Here in Acts, Peter is doing the healing, not Jesus.* The truth of that welled up within me, and suddenly God poured into me the faith that "cometh by hearing." I now had something doctrinally concrete to hang onto. I had faith to believe that I could pray for SanDee's healing.

A few days after the surgery, discouragement returned. One afternoon when I was visiting SanDee at the hospital, the surgeon called me into the tiny counseling room.

He didn't beat around the bush as he told me the cold, hard facts. "We sent eleven samples of lymph nodes from your wife to be tested. Nine of the eleven were malignant. This puts her statistical chance for survival at zero. You should not delay in getting all your papers in order. Have your wife sign over to you anything that might be in her name only. That will keep you from having a lot of legal mess to go through later. I'm sorry. Do you have any questions?"

Well, at least I didn't have to wonder if he was keeping anything from me. Brutal frankness may have been best, but it surely was painful.

I went to the elders of the church because I had read, *"Is there any sick among you? let him call for the elders of the church; and let them pray over him, anointing him with oil in the name of the Lord; And the prayer of faith shall save the sick, and the Lord shall raise him up; and if he have committed sins, they shall be forgiven him"* (James 5:14,15).

The first elder said, "I'll be glad to pray, but we should be careful to pray for God's will. Maybe it isn't His will to heal SanDee."

The second elder said, "I hold to the interpretation that James is talking about spiritual healing, not physical. I couldn't pray for her cancer to be healed."

The third elder said, "I believe that James meant a literal, physical healing."

Back and forth their discussion went, but by this time I wondered how this group of elders could ever agree and pray "the prayer of faith." Finally, one of the men compassionately put his arm around my shoulder and told me that they would be standing with me when SanDee died. That was not what I wanted to hear, but it was the best thing that ever happened to me. I was driven into searching the Scriptures for myself and was to emerge with a deep and abiding faith.

As I read the many accounts of healing in the Bible, my faith in God's ability to heal, without any particular formula or person, grew. It seemed that the only common denominator in all the cases of healing was faith, and God had given me that.

Faith, but not peace, was mine. My nights were restless and fretful. I even stopped using the alarm clock. Every night, I woke many times in deep, fervent prayer for SanDee. I learned the truth of praying without ceasing. When it was time to get up for work, I was always awake.

Then one morning, I awoke a half-hour past the time to get up! A feeling of guilt overwhelmed me when I realized that I had slept the whole night through and had not prayed, even once, for SanDee.

"Oh God, forgive me for not praying for my wife," I implored. "I must have just gotten too tired."

*You don't have to pray any more; she's healed.*

That thought reverberated in my brain, until I knew beyond a doubt that God had spoken to me. It was the first time I had ever heard His voice.

Jubilantly, I shook SanDee awake. "Get up and fix breakfast! You're healed!" I exclaimed.

## Return to SanDee's Story

"Fix breakfast?" I asked disbelievingly. I groggily emerged from the stupor of deep sleep. Fix breakfast! I had just had two major operations and spent most of my time languishing in bed while others waited on me. "Jim," I inquired, "what do you mean?" The joy on my husband's face made me realize that something dramatic had happened.

"You're healed!" he exclaimed. "I know you're healed. God told me, so get up and fix my breakfast!"

Well, I didn't feel healed, and I didn't feel like getting up to fix breakfast, but a verse of scripture popped into my mind and I had no choice. *"Wives, submit yourselves unto your own husbands, as unto the Lord"* (Ephesians 5:22).

In obedience to my own husband, and to Jesus, whom I had vowed to obey, I painfully got out of bed and headed towards the kitchen. By the time I got there, the pain was gone, and there has never been another trace of cancer in my body from that day on.

God used my healing as a catalyst. It energized us with faith - not only in God's ability to heal, but faith that God's Word could be taken literally and that we could trust Him to do all that He promises in His Word. All of our life experiences from that time on are related to this one pivotal experience. Do I mind having lost a breast? My loss was great, but my gain has been so much greater.

My attitude was helped by some very important decisions I made in the early days after my surgery. When I realized that several items of clothing in my closet would never again be appropriate for me to wear, I got rid of them. I had just made a new white pique sundress before I went to the hospital. I had never had a chance to wear it and never would. It could remain in the closet as a constant reminder of what I wished I could wear, causing a "pity party" every time I looked at it, or it could be given away. I gave it away.

The other decision I made was to look outward to the needs of others. As soon as I was accepted, I joined the Cancer Society's Reach to Recovery program. Through that program, I was able to visit other mastectomy patients in the hospital to encourage them, teach them exercises to strengthen their arms, and generally be a support in a difficult time.

The scars in my body became an ever-present reminder of the touch of God upon our lives.

There have been so many wonderful healings in our family over the years. I often wondered if God allowed them to happen as a means of reaching my parents. In **I Corinthians 1:22a,** I read, *"The Jews require a sign....."* At the time of my healing, and other healings to follow, Mom and Dad were temporarily thrilled. All too soon though, their human intellect reasoned away the miracle with such statements as, "Other people have had cancer and lived," or "Maybe Jeff outgrew his eye problem." Grieving for their unbelief, I understood more clearly how people could walk with Jesus when He was here on earth, beholding His miracles first hand, and then turn away in doubt or unbelief.

**May 1972**

Surely this can't be true! The doctor was recommending a third operation on Jeff's eyes, and he wasn't yet nine years old. The previous two operations had been unsuccessful. *Would a third one be any better?* We wondered.

Jeff had been born with a birth defect in his eyes. Occasionally, we'd notice his eyes turning outward. When he started to walk, he'd bump into the edges of walls or furniture. Our concern took us first to our pediatrician and eventually to an eye specialist. The problem was diagnosed as defective coordination of the eyes, and surgery was scheduled when Jeff was two years old.

When the bandages were removed, Jeff's eyes were nice and straight. Our elation was short-lived, however. In three months, the eyes started to turn worse than ever. No explanation could be given by the doctor for the cause of the problem. Further testing revealed a nearsighted condition in addition to the focusing weakness. At this point, glasses were recommended to correct both problems.

People would ask, "Isn't it difficult to keep glasses on such a young child?" It wasn't. Jeff's vision was so poor without glasses that he became very dependent on them.

When he was four years old, surgery was suggested for the second time. We went through the same procedure; this time his eyes held for nine months. Imagine our dismay when they started to turn again! We next went into a series of  different methods designed to strengthen Jeff's eyes - patches, exercises, etc. Nothing helped.

By the time Jeff turned eight, it was discovered that he was using only one eye. To compensate for the double vision he was experiencing, his brain blocked out the vision in the other eye. If this continued, he'd eventually lose the sight in that eye. We began a program to try to "wake up" the sleeping eye and train it to work in conjunction with the other one. All of this was to no avail.

As a last resort, a prism was put on the lens of Jeff's glasses to further force his eye straight. The effect on him was horrible. He had extreme nausea, as he'd feel as though the ground were rushing up at him. Of course, this was affecting his school work, his personality, and his parents who loved him.

At this point, Jim said we needed to pray specifically for Jeff's healing, not just the routine praying we had been doing in family devotions.

One day, soon after, we were invited to a teaching conference in Miami, Florida. Jim and I attended with some friends. That night, after a wonderful day of being fed from God's Word, I felt the Lord speak to me. It wasn't in an audible voice, but I knew it was the Lord. *If you come back tomorrow night, I'll heal Jeff's eyes.*

The next morning at breakfast, Jim announced to the four children, "We're going to Miami tonight. God told Mom that he'd heal Jeff's eyes!"

We were trying desperately to walk in faith and to be obedient to everything we felt the Lord told us to do, so off we went.

By the time we arrived at the conference center, the meeting was in progress. We found seats close to the front in the crowded auditorium. About two thousand people were in attendance.

When the meeting ended, a young man in his twenties approached the speaker who was still standing at the podium and whispered something to him. Jim had already started toward the rear exit with the three older children. I was in my seat trying to wake Bonnie to put her shoes on. Both Jim and I were bewildered about what God was going to do for Jeff. The meeting was over, and nothing had happened that we could see; we were very disappointed.

About that time, the speaker returned to the microphone and announced, "Please give me your attention. This brother has something to say."

Jim, wanting to be polite, stopped and sat down with the children at the back of the auditorium. I was still seated, struggling with a knot in a shoelace.

"I've been battling with the Lord all night," the young man began." I feel that He told me there is someone here tonight who needs prayer for healing his eyes, and I'm to pray for him."

Wow! I looked back for Jim and saw him shoving Jeff back down the aisle toward me. I surely didn't feel disappointed now! At the eleventh hour, Jesus was going to answer our prayer!

When we reached the front of the auditorium with Jeff, the young man had stepped off the platform and was standing below. He told us that the Lord had healed his son's eyes and that had given him faith to believe for his own eyes to be healed. Now he was going to pray for our son. He then placed his hand on Jeff's head and prayed a simple prayer.

When we reached our car, our son Tim, then eleven years old, said, "Read the sign across the street without your glasses, Jeff."

Jeff took off his glasses and asked, "What sign?" He couldn't even see it.

"Mom, why can't Jeff see?" questioned Tim. "You said he'd be healed if we came here."

I had the reply ready! "The Lord told us to come, and we were obedient. He told me that He'd heal Jeff's eyes. We'll believe what we cannot see. It may be a week or a year until we see the results of our obedience, but I *know* God touched Jeff  tonight." We sat in the car, and together we thanked God for healing Jeff's eyes.

*"Now faith is the substance of things hoped for, the evidence of things not seen"* (Hebrews 11:1).

Two days later, Jeff, with his glasses off, was sitting in the kitchen staring at the wallpaper. "Mommy, why don't the flowers have a fuzzy line around them anymore?" he asked. This was the first sign of the miracle we were about to experience! Throughout that week, we watched as Jeff's eyes got straighter and straighter, and his glasses were on less and less.

By Friday, Tim was standing across the kitchen with a milk carton in his hand. "Read this word, Jeff," he challenged.

"I can't," Jeff replied.

"Well, spell it!" Tim answered, realizing that Jeff didn't know the word!

Jeff quickly began to read, "P-O-I-N-S-E-T-T-I-A. (That was the name of the dairy.) Jeff then proceeded to read down the milk carton, even reading the tiny letters, "one-half gallon," in the corner. Our hearts leaped for joy!

Now came the testing. Jeff's eyes were straight most of the time, not all, and he put his glasses aside. At this point, his faith carried *us*. Every day he prayed, "Thank you, Lord, for healing my eyes." One day he confessed, "My eyes are better than they used to be but not as good as they're going to be."

The most heart-rending episode for me was the day one of his eyes was all red and blood shot. I struggled with whether he should have taken his glasses off. I finally asked, "Do you want to put your glasses back on?"

Jeff looked quizzically at me. "Why?" he asked. "I just got some sand in my eye and it hurts. Could you put some eye-drops in it?"

Many people asked if we were going to take Jeff to the eye doctor. Their faith hinged on his report, even though they saw his eyes straight and his glasses off. We decided to wait for his regular appointment in August. That visit would certainly confirm the extent to which his eyes had been healed.

**August 10, 1972**

"Where are Jeff's glasses?" the technician asked. Having given me an answer, Jim had prepared me for this question before it was voiced.

"We don't think he needs them, but we'll let you decide," I replied. Jim didn't want the examination to be colored by any prejudice.

Miss Clark continued with the exam, running Jeff through a gamut of tests to check both his focusing and vision. On May 11, when he had his last examination, he could see only the big **E** on the chart without his glasses. He couldn't focus without them at all. Now, without glasses, he could read almost to the bottom of the chart and focused the full range.

"Jeff! Have you been eating carrots, or what!" Miss Clark exclaimed.

I happily related the story of his healing to her.

Looking bewildered, she left to get Dr. Weiner. It was a long time until he came into the room. When he did, his behavior was definitely out of character. Normally, he was very cordial and greeted

Jeff and me warmly. This time, he hurried in without a word, sat in a chair, and stared at the records in the folder on his lap.

After a long time, he spoke, "This couldn't be! If Jeff has been without glasses since May, his eyes should be much worse, not better. I have no medical explanation. Tell me what happened."

Miss Clark, who had come into the room, said, "I told you doctor; she said they just prayed!"

The moment to share with Dr. Weiner had arrived. This dear Jewish doctor listened to the whole story. *"The Jews require a sign..."* (I Corinthians 1:22a).

## November 11, 1976

It was a week when all kinds of little things went wrong. I had just finished complaining to Jim that I couldn't take one more thing when we heard a bloodcurdling scream from the front yard. It was one of those moments when you're scared to death to find out what happened, yet know you have to.

We ran out the front door to the hysterical cries of Loryn, Jeff, and Bonnie: "Timmy fell! Timmy fell!"

When Jim and I reached the area under the tall Australian pines, we found Tim lying on his back, not breathing, and turning blue. We fell on our knees in the dirt and called, "Jesus!"

In minutes, Tim began to breathe - labored, painfully - but he was breathing. With each breath, he gasped, "Jesus, help me." There is power in THAT NAME!

We discovered that Tim had climbed to the top of a tree. He called down to his sisters and brother, "I can see the traffic light (two miles away) on PGA Boulevard!" Then, the tree swayed in the wind and the top broke off, sending Tim, head-first, hurtling thirty-five feet to the ground. Half way down, a limb broke his fall, causing him to flip and land flat on his back.

Not considering the consequences, Jim asked, "Can you get up?" We helped Tim into the house, where he still was having difficulty breathing. "We'd better take him to the hospital," Jim suggested, "but call the prayer chain first."

Phone call made, we gently placed Tim in the back of our station wagon and left for the fifteen-mile trip to the hospital. All the way there, Jim prayed, "Lord, please heal anything that's broken." By the time we arrived at the hospital, several Christian men were already there to meet us and pray for Tim. How we appreciated the love of God expressed through these caring men.

When we drove up to the emergency room entrance, I went in to inform them that we had brought our son who had just fallen thirty-five feet out of a tree. They came out and gingerly lifted Tim onto a stretcher. We didn't have the heart to tell them that we had foolishly gotten Tim up on his feet after the fall!

After half-an-hour, X-rays had been taken and read. "How far did you say Tim fell?" the technician asked. When told again, thirty-five feet, he just shook his head. "Nothing's broken. He's one lucky kid!" he said.

Tim walked out of the hospital, a little sore, but well.

The next day, the hospital called and asked permission to re-X-ray Tim. After the dry reading, there was something questionable. We returned and Tim was X-rayed again. This time, the attending physician asked, "Was Tim ever involved in a car or sports accident that affected the vertebrae in his neck?

"No, he has never been in any kind of an accident," I replied.

The doctor showed me the dry X-rays from the day before, as well as the ones they had just taken. There was a healed fracture in Tim's neck.

We believe that God, in answer to prayer, healed Tim on the way to the hospital.

**June 1978**

"Please let us go to Jesus '78," Tim and Jeff begged." We can go with Mr. Conway. He invited us. All the boys from the youth group are going. Please!"

For the past few summers, a festival was held in Orlando. Well-known Christian speakers and music groups were brought in from all over the world for three days. We had attended one year and were impressed to see so many young people listening to good Bible teaching. Deciding it would be a good experience for the boys, we agreed to let them go. Mr. Conway would be sure to supervise them, and camping out would add to their fun. We expected them home on Sunday evening.

On Sunday at five-thirty, the phone rang. Jeff, at the other end, stammered out, "D-d-d-d-dad." He couldn't manage to say anything, and after a long pause, a girl took the phone from him.

"Mr. Stone, Tim's been burned badly and is on the way to Vero Beach Hospital. The radiator exploded on him."

Jim said, "We'll leave right away and be there as soon as possible!" We left immediately. Vero Beach was a two-hour drive from our house.

Jim, thinking of the agonizing pain of even a little burn, prayed all the way there for the pain to be removed. I was fighting a silent, mental battle with the devil. *Tim will never play the piano again; his hands are so burned. Tim will never paint again.* These thoughts tormented my mind as we sped along the Florida Turnpike.

After many minutes of entertaining these thoughts and bemoaning the fact that our multi-talented son would never play the piano or do art work again, I got angry at the devil. *Wait just a minute!* I thought. *I don't even know where Tim was burned. The girl just said that he'd been burned, not where the burns were.*

As quickly as those negative thoughts came and left, a scripture verse replaced them. *"Casting down imaginations, and every high thing that exalteth itself against the knowledge of God, and bringing into captivity every thought to the obedience of Christ"* **(II Corinthians 10:5).**

*Thank you, Lord. I will cast down imaginations.* From that time until we arrived at the hospital, I was free from the fearful thoughts the devil used to play havoc with my mind, and I could pray for Tim. The Bible says  "fear has torment," and that afternoon I realized how incapacitating fear can be. While I was entertaining fearful thoughts, I couldn't pray; all I could do was despair.

Arriving at the hospital, we were ushered into the emergency room where Tim was being treated. If I hadn't been so concerned about our son, I might have laughed aloud at the devil. Tim had bandages on his chest, his legs, and his arms - right up to, but stopping short of, his hands. His face was singed, and he had second and third degree burns on the other areas, but his hands were free - not a burn on them!

What an important lesson I learned that day. So many times after that, I remembered to "cast down imaginations" and deal only with truth when Satan tried to tell me lies.

We took Tim home, and on the way, he told us what had happened that afternoon. "Mr. Conway's van has the radiator between the driver's seat and the passenger seat," Tim explained. "We were headed home on the turnpike when the engine overheated. Mr. Conway pulled in at the Yeehaw Junction Plaza to wait for the van to cool before putting water in the radiator. When he thought it was cool enough, he asked me to slowly release the cap. I started to, when it suddenly exploded all over me. I jumped out onto the ground, and the guys with us took our cooler and threw the cold water on me. A crowd gathered, and two different people suggested other things to do. The first said to put ice on me. Someone got ice from the plaza restaurant and that was on a little while. Another person said to get the ice off and let the burns breathe. While they were working on me, the ambulance came to take me to the hospital. In the ambulance, they gave me a pain shot and applied saline solution. It hurt so bad, Mom and Dad. I'm afraid of when the shot wears off."

Before we left the hospital, we were given a prescription for pain medication, and the emergency room doctor told us to find a local doctor when we got home. "Tim will probably need plastic surgery on some of the worse areas," he said. By the time we arrived home, our pharmacy was closed for the night. We hoped that aspirins would help Tim until morning when we could get the prescription for pain reliever filled. Long after it was time for the original shot to have worn off, we realized that Tim had no pain. We never filled the prescription.

After several days, Jim wanted to take pictures of the burns. I resisted even the thought. They looked so awful. "Why in the world would you want to take pictures?" I pleaded.

"I just feel that I'm supposed to; I don't know why," Jim answered.

He took the pictures.

A week after the pictures were taken, we knew why. At the end of a week, he was completely healed. Where there had been raw hamburger-looking flesh a week before, there was now smooth pink skin. There were no scars anywhere.

We shared this story with two friends who were registered nurses. They both recognized the confused methods used to treat Tim at the turnpike plaza as the recommended medical procedure for treating burns!

We took another set of pictures to the glory of God.

These two incidents in Tim's life had a profound effect on him. At seventeen years old and a senior in high school, he applied for admission to Bethany Fellowship Missionary Training Center in Minneapolis, Minnesota. One of the admission requirements was to write his personal testimony. Tim wrote, "When I was seven years old, Dad read a book to me about missionaries. After reading it, we discussed what it meant to be a real Christian. That night, I made a decision to follow Christ, and my Dad prayed with me." He went on to tell in detail about the accidents he had had at fourteen and sixteen years old. His conclusion was that God had spared his life and healed him so that he would serve Him with his whole heart. Tim has done just that.

Although we would like to spare our children from some of the most difficult experiences on their path of life, we can trust them to their heavenly Father. He loves them so much more than we ever could and will work all things together for their good. *"And we know that all things work together for good to them that love God, to them who are the called according to His purpose"* (Romans 8:28).

## Chapter Four

## Acknowledging Him as Provider

*"But seek ye first the kingdom of God, and his righteousness; and all these things shall be added unto you"* (Matthew 6:33).

"Mom, there's nothing to eat!" eight-year-old Jeff whined. He was standing, peering into the pantry early one morning before breakfast.

Looking over his shoulder at the wide array of breakfast cereal on the shelf, I was amazed. "What do you mean, there's nothing to eat?" I asked. "There's Corn Flakes, Cheerios, Rice Krispies, Kix, and oatmeal!"

"But there's no Frosted Flakes," he lamented.

*Oh, Lord,* I inwardly prayed, *"How do we teach our children gratitude for your provision, when we have so much?*

Soon that prayer was to be answered, as we were launched out on a walk of faith I would never have believed possible.

### Jim's Story  Fall 1971

The group of system analysts and programmers I was managing for RCA had just finished a project. I was sitting at my desk, writing a letter to general management, tooting our horn over the great job we had done. A thought crossed my mind. *Do something with eternal value.* Where in the world did **that** come from?

After a couple of weeks, I was repeating the process, writing a letter about another completed project. Again, a thought contrary to what I was writing crossed my mind. *Within three years, no one will even remember this project. Why don't you do something of eternal value?* Could this be the Lord trying to get my attention?

Another peculiar event was taking place at the same time. Whenever I opened my Bible, the page seemed to turn to Matthew 6, and my attention was drawn to the thirty-third verse. *"But seek ye first the kingdom of God, and his righteousness; and all these things shall be added unto you. "* I had been struggling for days with all of this and had

had little peace. What had been happening seemed so strange to me that I shared the incidents with SanDee.

"I also seem to be reading **Matthew 6:33** a lot lately," she confessed. "What do you think it means?"

"Maybe I'm supposed to leave my job at RCA," I answered.

That thought persisted for days. Finally, I decided to get serious and fast and pray for three days, hoping for an answer. After all, I had a wife and four children to support, not to mention a hefty mortgage on the much larger house we had built a few years ago in Lake Park. I was not one to take foolish chances.

On my lunch hour I walked around a little lake on the grounds of RCA and I prayed, instead of eating. *What would I be doing if I left my job, Lord?"*

At the end of my three-day fast, the answer came. *If you knew where you are going and what you're going to be doing, it would be no more dramatic than any other job change. If, however, you walk out of RCA on the final day of your employment saying that you are following the leading of the Lord, that will stick in people's minds.*

With that, I had peace and assurance. The answer had come, and it made good sense. It would glorify God.

At the dinner table that night, I outlined to the family what I thought to be the leading from the Lord. "God has been speaking to me about leaving my job and trusting Him to satisfy our needs," I explained. "In **Matthew 6:33,** He promises to take care of us. We have a lot of things that God may not consider needs, and we may have to change our lifestyle. Bonnie, it may mean never having a two-wheel bike. It may mean skipping vacations or the circus or the fair. It may mean selling the house and moving into a tent." (The boys liked that one.) "It may mean eating nothing but lima beans." (The boys didn't like that one.) I told SanDee that we may have to leave our "dream house."

SanDee and I had decided to include the children in everything that affected the family. We wanted them to see the reality of God's hand in our lives. I wouldn't leave my career unless everyone individually counted the cost. I tried, as best as I could, to help each family member understand what leaving my job might mean. To make everyone feel a part of the decision, we voted. It was a secret ballot, which could be checked "yes" or "no." When the votes were counted, all six ballots had been checked "yes." We told the children not to discuss our decision yet, as I wanted God's timing for handing in my resignation.

Some months later, an odd thing happened. One night while building shelves at the Christian school our children attended, I was called to the phone. SanDee was on the other end. "Mr. Sarnoff (the president of RCA) was just on the news. He announced that the computer division is closing," she informed me.

"The computer division! That's us!" I exclaimed. Then I thought, *Lord, you didn't have to close down the entire division just to get me to leave! Really, I was planning to go!*

Quickly, I recalled how the still, small voice of God had been urging me to leave my data processing career. It had been almost a year since He first told me to "do something with eternal value."

The message was clear, but I was in the fifteenth year of a career I enjoyed. My status as manager with a generous salary, made the job situation very comfortable. *Maybe God does have to close down the entire division just to get me to leave,* I regretfully mused.

SanDee continued, "Isn't it exciting to know that God is doing something in our lives?"

The next few months saw several increments of layoff as the work force was pared down. After several months, management made a decision to keep a minimum number of employees at the plant in anticipation of future plant utilization. My supervisor told me that I had been chosen to stay. My heart sank. *I'm going to be here forever,* I envisioned. This was definitely confusing.

*God,* I prayed, *if I'm supposed to stay with the company, why the strong impression to leave?* The answer came back, crystal clear. *I want you to leave from a position of strength, not weakness.* I could see the value. In years to come, I could say I left my career at God's leading, not because I lost my job and had to find something else to do.

**September 1, 1972**

Wanting to be fair to RCA, I thought it would be appropriate to leave at the end of the year, allowing plenty of time to find and train a replacement.

When I told Frank, my boss, he reminded me of the substantial raise I was going to receive soon. (About two weeks prior to my resigning, Frank had confided that he had arranged a salary increase for me. I had thanked him warmly, knowing that I'd never spend a cent of it.) Along with the raise would come a grade increase, elevating my position in the company. This corresponded to a larger office overlooking the lake. I recognized that Satan was trying to entice me to stay, with the natural allurement of money and position. I knew that would thwart God's plan for my life. By now, God had given me a resolve in my heart and that insulated me against this temptation. I was learning that real security comes from faith in God's faithfulness.

**September - December 1972**

Something really strange began to happen after I turned in my notice at RCA. My records for our finances began to show a steady decline. It actually became necessary to defer payment of some bills. Since we had always paid bills immediately upon their receipt, it was particularly perplexing. We had incurred no new debts, my salary was higher than it ever had been, and we had no unusual expenditures.

The effect of this financial pinch began to show in the pantry, refrigerator, and deep-freeze. What had consistently looked like a small grocery store dwindled to a shadow of its former self !

"Remember when Jeff said 'there's nothing to eat' a few months ago?" SanDee reminded me. She had prayed at that time that we could teach our children gratitude. Here was our opportunity.

Secretly thinking that now there really wasn't much to eat, I had an idea. I told the children that as long as there was anything edible in the house, we couldn't say, "There's nothing to eat !"

At first, even for SanDee, creating meals from our meager stock was a challenge. Then came the day when SanDee informed us that the only thing remaining in the house was a collection of beef kidneys in the freezer. They had been stuck in the far recesses of the shelf as food for a dog we no longer had.

"Cook them for dinner," I said.

"Surely you've got to be kidding," SanDee replied.

"We're to eat everything edible in the house" (not being really sure that the kidneys qualified under the heading of edible).

That evening, I asked God's blessing on the food with a little more fervor than usual. The strange odor emanating from the pot on the stove didn't help my faith any. We had made such a big deal about gratitude for God's provision that no one dared to complain! I particularly remember twelve-year-old Loryn's face. It went through many involuntary contortions as she chewed the rubbery substance, yet she managed a weak, "M-m-m, Mom, this is good."

*What a liar!* I thought. Then the Lord chastised me with another thought. *Loryn's claiming by faith what she can't grasp in the natural.*

The kidney caper was one of the highlights in our learning to trust God for provision. We must have passed the test because we always had adequate and "normal" food after that. Moreover, our children never again complained that there was nothing to eat.

At this period in our lives, Satan was always around with discouraging thoughts. I was trying to learn to discern God's voice and direction and quickly came to the conclusion that God encourages, Satan discourages.

A discouraging thought: *If you can't even make ends meet on your RCA salary, how in the world are you going to make it on **nothing**?*

An encouraging thought: *You're experiencing the loaves and fishes in reverse. I wanted you to see that I can take nothing and make plenty, or plenty, and make nothing.*

Thanking the Lord for that valuable lesson, we watched our financial status steadily improve. By mid-December we were back on top of things.

*"Trust in the Lord with all thine heart: and lean not unto thine own understanding. In all thy ways acknowledge him, and he shall direct thy paths"* **(Proverbs 3:5,6).**

He truly was directing our paths.

As Frank escorted me to the door on the last work day in December, he told me that I could still change my mind. He'd create another job for me. As I turned to wave to him one last time, I remembered a scripture in **Genesis 12:1**, *"Now the Lord has said unto Abram, Get thee out of thy country, and from thy kindred, and from thy father's house, unto a land that I will shew thee..."* I yearned to see the land.

### Back to SanDee

When Jim walked out of RCA for the last time in December, 1972, he walked into total reliance on God and took the rest of the family with him. As we were faithful in our feeble human endeavor to *"seek first the kingdom of God,"* we found God faithful to abundantly fulfill his end of the bargain - *"and everything you need will be added unto you."*

We adopted a few simple philosophies as we searched the scriptures trying to be obedient to our part of seeking Him first.

1.    We would never again say, "we can't afford it."
      If what we thought was a need was not supplied,
      we'd accept that God thought it was a "want,"
      not a need. We could afford whatever He
      wanted us to have.

2.    Because of this new way of life, we would
      discard all credit cards.

3.    Based on **Philippians 4:6**, we would never tell
      anyone but God that we thought we had a need.
      *"Be careful for nothing; but in everything by
      prayer and supplication with thanksgiving, let
      your requests be made known unto God."*

4.    No matter what our pantry or financial state
      looked like, we would continue to entertain

guests. We were told in the Bible to "be hospitable."

Jim received a severance check from RCA. With it, we paid off all our debts - everything but our house mortgage. We had no debts, no money, and we also had no income. The fact that we were totally dependent on God became a stark reality.

On January 2, Jim got up, dressed, and started the day like any other workday. The difference was, he had no place to go! "I read in II **Thessalonians 3:10** that a man shouldn't eat if he won't work," Jim informed me. So he began to work, building bookshelves that we had always wanted in our family room.

One morning after the bookcase was completed, he received a phone call from the Christian school the children attended. "Loryn said you're not working. Could you possibly help us out by substituting for sixth grade today?" the secretary asked. Being eager to do anything that might be something the Lord was asking him to do, off to the academy he went! After a wonderful day with the students, he was a lot more joyful than I'd ever seen him after a day's work.

That first day led to many calls to substitute-teach that year. One day it could be kindergarten; the next, a calculus class in twelfth grade. Jim laughed, "Do you realize that I'm making in a week at the academy what I made in a day at RCA, yet our needs are being met? I think we're seeing the loaves and fishes. God is certainly multiplying our income!"

Concurrent with Jim's leaving his career was an announcement he made to a sharing group that had been meeting in our home on Friday nights. The purpose of this group was to share Christ with a group of young, truth-seeking adults. Most of them were unchurched and not willing to attend a conventional church. Many were coming out of the "hippie" movement and knew that their clothing style - jeans, T-shirts, sandals, and long hair on the men - would be unacceptable. Yet, many of them had accepted Christ in the past year. We were confident that He could change anything that He thought needed changing. Our job was to teach the Word and to love them as they were.

The sharing group was meeting a need for teaching and fellowship, but one meeting a week seemed inadequate. "Why can't we meet on Sunday?" Rob asked.

That started Jim thinking, *maybe we could.* At the last sharing group meeting in December, 1972, Jim announced, "My family and I are going to sit in our living room next Sunday morning to sing, pray, and read the Bible. The front door won't be locked, so anyone wanting to join us may feel free to do so." The following Sunday morning, the six of us gathered in the living room. To our utter amazement, twenty-five people joined us!

Our intellect made several attempts at questioning the wisdom of what we were doing, but all doubt was completely erased by the comfort of the Holy Spirit and by the encouragement of the people attending. Our church leaders, knowing that these young people weren't ready for a conventional church and seeing the good fruit in their lives, gave us their approval. That was important to us.

The group grew. Thirty... forty... fifty people crowded into our house. We moved from the living room to the family room so that the adjoining kitchen and screened-in porch could afford overflow space. We were glad to have a house big enough to accommodate all these people.

A phenomenon began to occur. Clothing and hair styles started to change. People confessed each week of habits they had been convicted of and had given up. More people began to be saved. One day, someone asked Jim to baptize him. Whew! He didn't think about all of these ramifications when we first opened our home!

Thinking that only a pastor could perform this function, Jim sought counsel from the church elders. They informed him that he already **was** a pastor. When he objected to even the idea, one of the men said, "You are feeding these people from God's Word; they look to you for leadership and counsel; what do you think a pastor is?" Regardless of how these men might have felt in the past, they knew that God was moving in a supernatural way, and they wanted to help. In the months to come, Jim was trained by them and was ordained to the Gospel ministry. The church in our home continued for seven years, until we moved away.

In the meantime, many of our original philosophies were tested. One of the first for me was continuing to entertain, whether we had money or not. At those times, I had to use whatever food was available in the house. The day soon came when company was coming for dinner, and we had no money. I scrounged up some stew beef, tomatoes, carrots, and onions. There was a box of saltines in the pantry. *Guess we're having stew,* I thought. *Sure would be better with potatoes in the stew and homemade bread to eat with it. Oh, well. At least I don't have to serve kidneys!*

A couple of hours before our guests were due, the stew was simmering on the stove. The doorbell rang and when I answered it, I found my mother-in-law standing there with a big grocery sack in her arms.

"Quick, take this!" she begged, "It's heavy."

Imagine my astonishment when I took the bag from her and realized that it was full of potatoes!

"You drove twenty miles to bring me a sack of potatoes?" I asked.

"Well," she replied, "you won't believe this crazy story!"

I could hardly wait to hear it, but first I peeled potatoes and gratefully added them to the stew.

Mom continued, "My sister-in-law is visiting from Indiana and was driving behind a big produce truck. All of a sudden, the back door of the truck flew open and a bushel of potatoes fell out. The bag broke, scattering potatoes everywhere. Well, the truck rolled on, the driver unaware of what had happened. Aunt Joan just couldn't let those potatoes go to waste, so she stopped to gather them. Then she had a good laugh at herself! What in the world would she do with potatoes, she was on vacation! *I'll just take them to Pat,* she thought. When she did, I knew that Dad and I couldn't use them, so here I am!"

"The Lord even gave me the desire of my heart," I told her, rejoicing.

Mom visited a while and left before the "going home" traffic was too bad. She wasn't gone very long before the doorbell rang again. This time it was my friend Alexis. "I'm on the way to my sister Barbara's for dinner." she said. "I made some homemade bread to take to Barbara and decided to make a loaf for you." *Oh, Lord, you are so good to us.* How I praised Him for caring about even the most minute details of my life.

When Jim left RCA we wondered how would God meet our needs, and what would He consider a need? Would He supply just bare essentials or things we would like to have, too?

We had two old cars at the time Jim left his career. We knew we could do without the luxury of two vehicles, but the "best" one was our immediate concern. It had 112,000 miles on it, and we knew it couldn't last forever.

A few months after Jim left RCA, a friend called. "Say," Pat began, "could you use another car? A friend of mine is moving to Minneapolis and wants to sell his Chevy station wagon for only $500. It has half the mileage of yours and four new radial tires."

Gulping, Jim remembered our pledge to tell God only a need, and he replied, "We'll pray about it and let you know by Saturday." It was Wednesday. Jim knew that we had $100 to our name!

"Lord, I'd sure like to be able to buy that car," Jim prayed. "We need $400 by Saturday." Suddenly an inspiration hit him! "Why don't we put our car in front of the house with a "FOR SALE" sign on it. We can ask for the $400 we need. That'll give the buyer a good deal. I think our car would list for at least $700. By not advertising, it will have to be the Lord if it sells."

The first day passed, and one person stopped to look at the car. He didn't want it. We continued to pray. Friday came, and it was my turn to pray during our morning family devotions. "Lord, help us get rid of our car."

No one stopped that day. Secretly, I was disappointed. *That car would have been a good deal, but the Lord knows best,* I tried to console myself.

That evening we went to our weekly sharing group. It was being held in someone else's home this week. Usually, the meeting was over at nine o'clock, but we became involved in a lively discussion with a new person, and it was close to ten-thirty when we headed wearily home.

As we approached our house on the dark road, I noticed that the car we had left in front of the house was in a different position from the way we had left it. Then our headlights caught the front end of the car in its beam, and I screamed, "Jim, the car's smashed!" Turning around, Jim shined the lights on the car in the yard. The whole front end was torn up and facing at a crazy angle.

"Oh no!" I exclaimed. "There's a car in the bushes!"

Jumping out, my heart thumping, I crawled through the thick palmettos to the car nestled between two trees, headlights still on. Peering in the darkness, I saw the form of a woman slumped over the steering wheel. I could vaguely determine in the darkness that her car was badly damaged.

*Oh, God! She's DEAD!* I feared. The car window was open, and I anxiously whispered, "Are you all right?" I really didn't expect a reply.

The woman raised up, however, and slurred, "Jus' a minute, lady. I jus' pulled off to rest.....I'll move." With that, she reached down to start the stalled engine. She had no idea of where she was, or that she wasn't going anywhere in her disabled car.

Maybe being so intoxicated was to her advantage. She wasn't injured at all! By this time, Jim had joined me, and we convinced her to let us help her walk into our house. She was still trying to convince us that she was going to drive off! She honestly didn't know what had happened.

Jim called the sheriff while I tried to coax our uninvited guest to tell me her name. When she finally did, I recognized the last name as being the same as a neighbor's on the next street. As soon as the phone was free, I called. The neighbor turned out to be the woman's son. He said he'd be right over. The sheriff came, made his report, and left.

We were amazed at the irony of the situation. Loryn had met the family. They were new in the neighborhood and had small children. Always on the lookout for potential baby-sitting jobs, our daughter had recently introduced herself. Loryn had suggested that we pray for them, since she suspected that the husband might have an alcohol problem. To honor her burden, we had been praying.

Now, he and his inebriated mother were sitting in our home. What an amazing answer to prayer! I'm sure that the Lord's concern was for this family's souls, and we had a wonderful opportunity to share Jesus with them.

Equally amazing was the answer to my prayer that morning, "Lord, help us get rid of our car!" I didn't suggest how, and His creativity optimized the current situation. God certainly is an economist, we learned. Why answer only one prayer when He can answer two! The woman's insurance company wrote a check to us the next day for $445!

Jim called Pat. "Tell your friend we'll take the car! You'll never believe what happened!" He went on to tell Pat about our prayer for the money, trying to sell our car, and the story of the drunk woman who had driven twenty-two miles until she got to the front of our house and smashed our car sitting in the yard. "Less than half a block more, and she would have been home!" Jim exclaimed. "The insurance money will pay for the new car and its registration!"

Those early days of learning to walk by faith were exciting. It was a time of seeing the promise of **Matthew 6:33** literally fulfilled in every realm of our being - spirit, soul, and body - everything we needed was adequately supplied. Spiritually, we were growing in leaps and bounds; intellectually, we were thrilled as we saw our needs met. God's ability and willingness to heal our bodies was awesome to us. We felt like little children who could just rest peacefully in their father's provision. Our lives were so free from everyday cares of the world.

God never seemed to run out of creative ways to supply our needs. When our funds were low, we saw Him provide in such unique ways that we could never outguess Him.

I sewed for people in order to help with the children's tuition at the academy. Never advertising for business, it was necessary to trust the Lord to send customers. It was also necessary to trust that I'd finish their garment, and it would be paid for in time for the tuition payment. In those times that I didn't have a sewing order or a dress wasn't picked up and paid for, God's creativity took over. We were to depend on Him totally, not on any human resource. Jim's substitute teaching salary and a small allowance from the church couldn't possibly cover our normal household expenses.

One time after a church service in our home, Jim was collecting the song books. What he thought was a bookmark turned out to be a $100 bill! We never discovered the source of this blessing (other than God), but it met a $100 need.

Another time, one of the ladies I sewed for died. In her will, she stipulated that I be given money for a month's tuition for the children.

When God thought we were in need of a car, we knew we could trust Him to provide. One of our many car stories involves a couple who had been in our church in Florida and had moved to Plano, Texas. They were back in the Palm Beaches for a visit about the time our Chevy station wagon was suffering from old age. Ernie and Dolores took us out for dinner. While we were eating, they kept grinning at each other as though they shared a wonderful secret. We were wondering what the private communication meant, when Dolores asked, "Ernie, are you going to tell them?"

Ernie smiled, "We have a car in Texas that we'd like to give to you. Could you use it?"

Could we ever! Now it was time for Jim and me to exchange glances! We really needed the car they offered, but it was in Texas and we were in Florida - without money to get it. We each silently shot up an arrow prayer for help!

However, Ernie wasn't through with his plan. He continued, "We really want you to see our new home, so after we get back, we'll arrange for plane tickets for both of you to fly out as our guests. Then, after visiting us, you can drive the car home. How's that?"

"Thank you, Ernie! Thank you, Lord!"

We drove that car, a Chevrolet Impala, for many years. We probably would have driven it for many more, except for an untimely accident that ended its life.

### Highland, New York  September 8, 1980

God has creative ways of both getting rid of and supplying cars. For many years, we had to be content with His choosing what we drove and His timing in the provision. We had recently moved to New York. One day, while he went to work, Jim had parked our Impala on a downtown street in Poughkeepsie, New York. When he returned to the car to drive home, he found it severely damaged. A note under the windshield wiper said, "Please call the Mountain View Bus Company." A phone number was on the note.

When Jim called, he was informed that a bus driver had parked an empty bus in a parking lot directly across the street from where our car was parked. The driver failed to secure the brakes, and the empty bus rolled down a slight incline right into our empty car.

By this time, our car was so old that it was declared "totalled" by the insurance company. They paid $350 for it, hardly enough to replace the only car we owned at the time.

Highland is on the west bank of the Hudson River; Poughkeepsie is four miles directly across on the east bank. Jim walked home that evening. The next morning, he walked back. The walk took him over the Mid-Hudson bridge spanning the river and downhill through a rock cut in the hills. That made the walk uphill on the way home, after a day's work.

"What can I pray for, God," Jim asked, wanting direction. The answer he seemed to get was, *Pray for a nice, economical car.*

During that time, we were in the habit of putting prayer requests on index cards, shuffling them, and distributing them around the breakfast table each morning. Then we'd take turns praying for the needs on the cards. When a request was satisfied, we'd remove that card, adding new ones when necessary. This day, Jim added a card to the pile. "A NICE, ECONOMICAL CAR."

A car was a *need,* wasn't it? We didn't know how this need would be met, but we anticipated a swift answer. Were we ever shocked! God's timetable definitely differed from our expectations. Every day we prayed for a nice, economical car. Every day, Jim continued to walk to Poughkeepsie and back. Occasionally, someone he knew would pass by and pick him up, but for the most part, he walked both ways. The days turned into weeks, and cold weather was soon to come. We kept praying, and Jim kept walking. One week...two weeks....three weeks....four weeks.....five weeks.....six weeks.....on he walked.

I was getting disheartened. October brought the chilly wind channeling up the Hudson River and snaking its icy tentacles up the rock cut toward Highland. Could my Florida-raised husband withstand the New York cold?

Then, God allowed one of his "little helpers" to talk to me! "Why is Jim so stupid?" a man in our church asked me. "Why doesn't he buy a car on time like a 'normal' person?"

*Maybe he's right,* I thought. In a split second, I began to entertain terrible thoughts about my husband. I felt so vulnerable. *If he looks stupid to other people, why bother? God always supplied our needs before, but maybe Jim's being presumptuous this time. I'm tired of walking by faith. I'd like to be" normal"!* It's amazing how many discouraging thoughts can attack your mind in a few minutes.

*Discouragement is from the devil.* That idea interrupted my rambling thoughts. I was brought back to encouraging thoughts of the abiding faith my husband had. God was our source of supply. Regardless of the way I felt or what this Christian man said, I would stand with my husband. We had been trusting the Lord together in this walk of faith for eleven years now, and God hadn't failed us yet.

In a few days, a friend called Jim. "Someone offered me a free car, and I don't need it," Mike said. "Maybe it's the car God has for you. Want to look at it?"

Jim did look at it and came home depressed. He told me about the car. "The car was old, worn, and got ten miles a gallon. I didn't want to be ungrateful, but after evaluating it for thirty minutes, I realized that it wasn't *nice,* and it definitely was not *economical.* It would have been immediate transportation, but I don't think it's what God has for us."

Jim was weary of walking, but on he trudged for yet another week. At the end of the seventh week, our friend Dan called from Florida. "Say, SanDee, could you give me the brownie recipe you made when I visited you last summer? They were so good." Flattered. I read the recipe to him, and then we chatted to catch up on the news. In the course of conversation, I told Dan about our wrecked car. "Could you use a little Subaru station wagon?" Dan asked. "I bought a new van for my carpet cleaning business, and I don't need a little car any more. It's only a few years old and gets thirty-four miles a gallon."

Not many days later, my friend Mary and I flew to Florida. We visited family and friends while there and drove the Subaru home. It was unquestionably nice and extremely economical! This was God's provision. Had we accepted the temptation of the other car, for convenience, we would have missed God's best.

### Florida Summer 1974

When Jim left RCA, friends, family, and acquaintances all wondered how we were going to send four children to college? We had no college fund, or any other funds, for that matter. Our only reply was that we trusted God to provide for the future. If college was in His plan for any or all of the children, that need would also be met. In the Lord's prayer, we ask Him to "Give us this day our daily bread"; we didn't need college money yet.

An interesting circumstance showed us how capable God is of working in every aspect of our lives.

My friend Beb's father was very ill in northern Minnesota. She really wanted to go to be with him and her mother. Her husband couldn't take time away from his business, so Jim suggested that I accompany her, along with her two boys and our children. "It's been kind of a rough year for you," Jim said. "Perhaps you could help out at Camp Joy while Beb's visiting with her folks. That way, maybe the kids could go to camp."

Camp Joy was a Christian summer camp for children. The directors spent their winters in Florida and had become our dear friends. When I called them, they were delighted at the prospect of my working at camp. "You can be in charge of the counselors." I was told.

We drove to Minnesota in Beb's little pickup, piling all six kids in the camper shell. It was a summer full of adventure, but most of all, it provided an answer to the college question for our two oldest children and provided direction for their future.

Most of the counselors were college students. Several of them really impressed me with their spiritual maturity. I learned that those students were from Bethany Fellowship, a missionary training school in Minneapolis.

When camp days ended, one of the Bethany students invited us to stop in Minneapolis on the way home for a tour of the school. I was impressed enough by the godliness of the students' lives that I asked Beb if we could visit Bethany. On the tour, we were told that Bethany is a work/study program. The students worked in several businesses on campus to pay for their own room and board and tuition. I was impressed; Loryn was even more so! "This is where I want to go to college," she informed me. Loryn still had two more years of high school. I nonchalantly answered, "We'll see."

In September, 1976, Loryn was enrolled at Bethany. Three years later, Tim was to follow her as a Bethany student. God even cared about college tuition!

## October 1976

Most of the time, God left us waiting until the last minute for an answer to prayer. We could never lean on our own understanding. He was directing our paths, and all we had to do was follow.

I received an invitation to my twentieth high school reunion in Hartford, Connecticut. It was the first invitation to a reunion I had ever received, and I really wanted to go. Having lost touch with most of my classmates, few knew that I had become a Christian. I hoped for a chance to share my testimony with anyone who would listen.

Everything was set for the trip. Jim thought it was a wonderful idea for me to fly to Connecticut for the long reunion weekend, and a former teacher invited me to stay in her home. There was only one crucial ingredient missing - money for a plane ticket! I made reservations in faith. I could pay for the ticket at the airport when I left.

We began praying for money. On the day before I was to leave, there were still no extra funds. The mail was my last hope! I anxiously waited for the mail delivery that day. As a matter of fact, I was standing next to the mailbox when the mail carrier drove up. I was secretly hoping some long-lost relative had left me an inheritance! Handing me one piece of mail, the mailman drove off, leaving me with an envelope in my hand. "The Revlon Company" was printed in the upper left-hand corner. *Phooey,* I thought. *Who needs junk mail at a time like this.*

I **really** wanted to go to the reunion! Uninterested, I tore open the envelope. Taped to a card were three shiny quarters - a shampoo refund. I could hardly get to Connecticut on that!

When Jim returned from work, he cheerfully inquired, "Well, did you get your money?"

I felt like hitting him! Instead, I held out my hand with the three quarters in my palm and moaned, "These came in the mail. It's not quite enough!"

Laughing, he replied, "Well, they look like seeds. Why don't you try planting them in the tithe box to see if they grow!"

"Are you serious?" I asked.

"Very," Jim replied.

Church was meeting in our home, and the tithe box was kept in a cabinet in our family room. I opened the door and listened as the three coins fell, plink..plink..plink.., to the bottom. Truthfully, I felt a little foolish!

A short time later, the doorbell rang. Opening the door, I found my friend Beb. I hadn't seen her in ages. "Come on in!" I greeted her.

"I can't," she replied. "I've got to get home for dinner, but I felt strongly that I was to give you this - right now!" She handed me a piece of paper and left. When I unfolded the paper, I found that it was a check made out to me for $100. That was half of the plane fare.

By nine o'clock that night, two more people "just happened" to drop in and share a gift of money. By bedtime, the exact amount needed was in my possession. The three seeds had quickly sprouted into three gifts!

### Highland, New York 1980

Twenty-two years in Florida never got the love of the four seasons out of my system. Whenever we'd vacation in the north, I'd admire all the stately old homes, rolling hills, high mountains, and the abundance of tall deciduous trees. Through the years, I was content to live in Florida, but once in a while, I'd dream about someday having a two-story northern house with a fireplace.

"Why don't you move to New York, buy a big house, and take girls from the program to live with you," Loryn suggested. She was working at the Walter Hoving Home in Garrison, New York, as part of her college training. Students at Bethany spent the first two years on campus, the third year away for practical training in home or foreign missions, and the senior year back at school. Loryn was chosen to work at this Christian drug and alcohol program.

Loryn tried to convince us of the needs for some of the girls leaving the program. "Mom and Dad, so many girls can't go back to their old environment. It would be wonderful if they could live with a Christian family and have a positive influence and example," she implored.

Living in New York gave me the northern home I dreamed of. We bought a Victorian farmhouse built in 1873. It had two stories, a fireplace, and one-hundred-year-old maple and pine trees shading its columned porches. It sounds romantic, but this house brought a whole new realm of trusting the Lord into our lives. Even the realtor who sold us the house tried to discourage us! It needed so much work. All we could see was the relatively low price, the potential for accommodating lots of people in its large rooms, and an opportunity to be completely out of debt.

Six months after moving in, an angry neighbor knocked on the door. "Your septic is backing up near my swimming pool," he yelled.

Shocked, we looked at the rancid water seeping up out of the ground and slowly creeping down a slope toward his yard. Apologizing profusely, we promised to do something immediately. We called a company to pump the septic tank, but to our dismay, we were informed that there wasn't one. Instead, there was an ancient cesspool, adequate for the one elderly lady who had lived there alone, but not for the number of people we now had living in the house. The cesspool was pumped out that day; a temporary reprieve, we were told. The needed septic system would cost over one thousand dollars!

"Lord," we prayed, "this is a high priority need! We want to be good neighbors."

Ginger, our Irish setter, had recently given birth to eight puppies. "Let's ask $150 for each for them," Bonnie suggested with youthful enthusiasm. *No one will pay that for them,* I thought. Nonetheless, we placed an ad in the local paper, and the puppies sold quickly at our asking price. This time, God used a dog to meet our need!

There were a thousand needs surrounding that old house, but one by one we saw each supplied in God's time, as we lovingly restored our home to its grandeur of bygone days. We never went into debt, yet so many times it would have been the easy way out. By now, faith in God's ability to provide, and the patience to wait, was a way of life. Even the hard times were exciting exercises of faith as we eagerly anticipated God's provision.

Our home became a haven for people torn by the storms of life. We thought we'd be ministering to girls from the Walter Hoving Home, but God always had a way of enlarging our borders. We learned to open our home and our lives to anyone the Lord sent. Many times, it was girls, but He also sent their children or husbands who needed help. Many came for a visit; others, for weeks, months, or longer. Joshua and Richard came forever.

Opening our lives to people has had its bitter-sweet experiences. Some of the  stories of people who yielded to the Lord and were redeemed from the power of sin are joyful. Others made all too real the truth that Jesus shared in **John 16:33,** *"In the world, ye shall have tribulation."* Fortunately, that isn't the end of the verse. He goes on to say, *"But be of good cheer, I have overcome the world."* Jesus has been our strength to deal with each discouraging situation.

A wise lady once told us, "Concentrate on those who yield to the Lord. Those who don't, turn over to Him. It'll help you not to be discouraged and thus, ineffective."

God chose a natural means to meet some of our needs for taking care of the people living with us. Jim was offered a job with the Department of Social Services as a systems analyst. After leaving his career in Florida, he never again expected to be in data processing. This time, however, was different. The motivation wasn't to build a career; the job was a means of supporting our family and others who had no income.

Pastoring was something else Jim layed down when we moved to New York. Thinking that our ministry would be to people living with us, we joined a local church and settled in. Jim was content for two years, but one day he confessed to me, "I feel like I have a pastor's heart, without a church to pastor."

One evening about three weeks later, Jim and a friend visited a men's meeting of another church. Addressing Jim, the group of men admitted that they had a leadership crisis. He was shocked when they went on to ask him to pastor their church. They had heard him teach, and two of the men had done a reference check on him. He joyfully accepted the call, and ministered to the church until moving out of state several years later.

Through the years, God has continued to meet our needs. To date, we have never bought a family car with our own money. In 1987, an unexpected inheritance allowed us to purchase a brand-new Plymouth Voyager mini-van.

### Huntsville, Arkansas  August 1993

After 182,000 faithful miles, the needed repairs on the van exceeded our available funds. By this time, we were living in a remote area in Arkansas and traveling a lot on speaking engagements. We felt that  dependable transportation was a need, and we hoped the Lord would agree. One day we asked Him, and that night we received a long-distance phone call informing us of a financial gift that was in the mail to us. When it arrived, it was enough to buy a new Oldsmobile Cutlass Supreme. We are so grateful, as we look forward to many miles of carefree driving.

*"Now unto him who is able to do exceedingly abundantly above all that we ask or think according to the power that worketh in us"* (Ephesians 3:20).

When Joshua was little, Bonnie taught him a chorus. It aptly expresses our praise to our God:

> My God is so big,
> So strong and so mighty,
> There's nothing my God
> Cannot do!

## Chapter Five

## Acknowledging Him as Teacher

*"....he shall teach you all things, and bring all things to your remembrance..."* (John 14:26)

### Lake Park, Florida 1969

"Why don't **you** pray; **you're** the one God talks to!" was Jim's reply to my suggestion that we pray about a current concern. He wasn't being sarcastic, just factual.

At another time, my pride would have silently agreed with him, and I would have prayed. However, this time, the words cut right to my heart. *That's not the way it should be, Lord. Jim should hear you speak to him for our family, not me.*

As quickly as I could, I excused myself. Going into the bathroom where I'd be assured of privacy, I fell to my knees and relinquished all my self-imposed rights to any spiritual leadership in the family. If God never spoke to me again, or taught me anything, I was willing. I just wanted Him to speak to Jim.

Jim was raised in church. Sick or well, day or night, winter or summer - as a child, he was there with his parents every time the church doors opened. Christianity was presented as a checklist of things you don't do. The emphasis on rules was so predominant that he never remembered hearing about the love of God or of the need for a personal relationship with Jesus Christ.

Jim's childhood impression was that God lived in the church building and you visited Him on Sunday morning and evening and on Wednesday night. He never realized that Christ can live in you and is there wherever you take Him. When he was given a choice as a teenager, he stopped going to church and set about to do everything that was on the "don't" list.

For me, coming to Christ as an adult had great value. There were no man-made rules to overcome. Jesus became a living presence in my heart from the start. The Bible became my rule book, and the Lord became my teacher. Loving Him, I wanted to obey.

Even after Jim accepted Christ, his negative childhood experiences with "religion," instead of a relationship with Christ, plagued him for many years. Attending church meetings was not met with the enthusiasm I had.

Our personalities were quite different, too. Jim, a quiet, introverted man, was content to let his enthusiastic, gregarious wife assume the spiritual leadership in our home. I was the one who encouraged devotions, church attendance, and fellowship with other believers. Without realizing it, I was trying to "help" God mold my husband. I finally understood that God didn't need **my** help. I needed **His.**

Now I really wanted to get out of the way. I vaguely remembered reading some passages of scripture that defined God's desired qualities for a godly woman. One morning after Jim left for work and the children left for school, I poured a cup of coffee, sat at the kitchen table, and opened my Bible to **I Peter 3:1-4.** As I read, some thoughts were indelibly imprinted on my brain.

*"Likewise, ye wives, be in subjection to your own husbands that, if any obey not the word, they also may without the word be won by the behavior of the wives."*

*Wow! My job is to be an example by how I live, not by what I say!*

I read on, *"While they behold your chaste conduct coupled with fear; Whose adorning, let it not be that outward adorning of braiding the hair, and of wearing of gold, or of putting on of apparel, But let it be the hidden man of the heart in that which is not corruptible, even the ornament of a meek and quiet spirit, which is in the sight of God of great price."*

My mind immediately went back to a time I had been invited to a fashion show by one of my wealthy Palm Beach sewing customers. It was held in an exclusive country club. As I glanced around the room at the elegantly coifed and beautifully attired older women, I was struck by the emptiness on their faces. These women had all that the world had to offer, yet most of them seemed to be stunningly painted and dressed hard shells. By contrast, I mentally reviewed some of the most beautiful older women I knew. They had no material wealth to speak of, or elegant clothes to wear, yet the softness in the lines of their faces and the peace reflected in their eyes came from years of walking close to Jesus.

*Oh, Lord. Let the beauty of Jesus be seen in me. Help me to develop a meek and quiet spirit,* I prayed. *Help me to get out of Jim's way and let you work in his life.*

The answer to that prayer was one of the lines on the blank contract I signed when I became a Christian. Had I known what was ahead, I might never have signed it!

Not too many months later, I lay in a hospital bed, diagnosed with terminal cancer. Now I was really out of the way! Sickness, and the prospect of imminent death, had a way of making me quiet!

Without any influence from me, Jim was able to have a deeply intimate encounter with Jesus. As he sought God for answers for my healing, two miracles unfolded. *"Seek and ye shall find,"* Jesus said. Jim sought, and he found - not only physical healing for me, but the necessity for him to make a real commitment to the Lordship of Christ. Suddenly, the introvert became an extrovert - alive with the good news of a God who answered his prayers and had spoken to him personally.

During my months of recuperation, my own personal miracles unfolded. First, my healing became a reality as a result of Jim's prayers. Secondly, God worked into my life a meek and quiet spirit. That, to me, was the greater miracle.

The first, my physical healing, took nothing on my part other than yieldedness to what Jim heard from God. His faith, and God's answer, took care of the rest.

The second required my attention. It meant keeping out of the way, being quiet, and coming under my husband's leadership. There was no struggle. I was now a broken vessel and could allow the beauty of Jesus to shine through.

With pride in my own spirituality now dead, I could see more clearly how to properly encourage Jim. When we had guests, it had been easy for me to lead the conversation. Jim, never wanting to interrupt, would wait for a break. If that break never came at the right time, the conversation would have changed subjects before he ever had an opportunity to say anything. By then, the relevance of what he was going to say was lost, so he kept quiet. As I determined to be sensitive, I learned an easy method of drawing Jim into the conversation. A simple, "What do you think, Jim?" was all it took to give him the floor.

What I "gave up" on my knees on my bathroom floor, I've gained a hundred-fold. The years since have been the reward. I have a husband who is the spiritual leader in our home, a pastor and elder in the churches we have attended, and a godly example to our children and grandchildren.

Jim would be the first one to share this secret with you today - he's where he is spiritually because I got out of the way and let God through!

God never stopped speaking to me when I asked Him to. He just got my attention in a dramatic way, and I learned to properly listen to Him. He taught me the truth about my position in the family. Learning about my role as a wife in God's order for the family has been the greatest lesson the Lord has taught me in my whole Christian experience.

This truth not only revolutionized our home but became a valuable tool in years to come, as God opened doors for me to teach other women their role in His order for the family.

*"Show me thy ways, O Lord; teach me thy paths. Lead me in thy truth, and teach me; for thou art the God of my salvation; on thee do I wait all the day."* (Psalm 25:4,5)

One of the first questions I ask when teaching women is, "Who has first place in your family?" Some of the Christian women schooled in submission would most likely answer, "My husband, of course."

The "liberated" woman-of-the-world would retort, "I've got my rights. I'm just as important as my husband!"

Then there are those who, if they're totally honest, would answer, "The children. Our home revolves around them."

The Lord taught me who He considers to be in first place - **all** of the above.

The husband is first place - in his place. Only he can assume the role of authority in the home. God gave it to him **(Ephesians 5:23).** He is responsible for the protection of his wife and children. He is to hear God's directions for the welfare of the family.

The wife is first place - in her place. She is the helper to her husband **(Genesis 2:18)**, keeper of their home **(Titus 2:5)**, and co-instructor of the children **(Proverbs 1:8)**.

The children are first place - in their place. This is the most protected spot in the family! A child has only one responsibility - obedience to his parents. A child does not have to make decisions, just follow them.     **(Ephesians 6:1-3)**.

Together, all three make up the unity of the family - different roles and functions, but each vital to the welfare of the whole. The Christian family should be a beautiful reflection of the unity of the Godhead. God, the Father; God, the Son; and God, the Holy Spirit - each with different roles, but united as One. God, the Father sent Jesus, the Son, who became obedient to everything the Father told him to do - even to death on the cross. Jesus ascended into Heaven and sent His Spirit, willing to indwell us and lead us into all truth. All first place - all God.

One time, I made up a little chart to place on the front of our refrigerator (See illustration). On a sheet of colored paper, I glued three offset white clouds at the top. In the center of the left cloud was "God." In the center of the middle cloud was "Jesus," and in the cloud to the right was "Holy Spirit."

Under the Jesus cloud was a short line attached to a circle with Jim's picture on it. Under that circle was another short line and a circle with my picture. Then, a line leading from Jim's circle and mine to an oval at the bottom with a picture of our children. At the sides were arrows representing Satan's fiery darts, which are ineffective if each member is in his protective circle.

**This poster was a graphic reminder to our family
of God's order for our home.**

*"I would have you know that the head of every man is Christ;
and the head of the woman is the man; and the head of Christ is God"*
(I Corinthians 11:3).

*"Wives, submit yourselves unto your own husbands, as it is fit
in the Lord. Husbands, love your wives, and be not bitter against them.
Children, obey your parents in all things; for this is well-pleasing unto
the Lord"* (Colossians 3:18-20).

As I studied the lives of some of the women of the Bible, I was astounded to read about some disastrous effects of women who took things into their own hands - things that are affecting our lives even now.

I read of Eve in the garden of Eden. As I reviewed the Genesis account of creation, I was amazed to discover that Eve wasn't even created when God gave the instructions to Adam.

*"And the Lord God commanded the man, saying, Of every tree in the garden thou mayest freely eat; But of the tree of the knowledge of good and evil, thou shall not eat of it; for in the day thou eatest thereof thou shalt surely die"* (Genesis 2:16,17).

It was easy for me to picture Adam, relaying God's instructions to Eve, as he wagged his finger in her face for emphasis, *"We must not eat the fruit of the tree in the middle of the garden. Eve, don't even touch it!"*

Then, Satan (in the form of a serpent) asked Eve, *"Yea, hath God said, Ye shall not eat of every tree of the garden?"*

What if Eve had answered, "Go ask my husband; he's the one God spoke to." Instead, she succumbed to a dialogue with the devil and ultimately cooperated in plunging mankind into sin.

I was so grateful to learn that in my protected place under my husband's covering, I can simply say, "Go ask my husband!"

I read about Sarah and Abraham **(Genesis 16-21)**. God spoke to the husband, Abraham. He promised him that he would be the father of a great nation. The problem was, Sarah was barren. Instead of trusting God and the word her husband had received from Him, Sarah persuaded Abraham to have a child by her maid, Hagar. She thought she was helping God. Abraham listened to his wife, and he did have a son, Ishmael, by Hagar.

God had promised Abraham that of his seed would come a great nation. God always keeps His word, so of the seed of Ishmael, the Arab nations were born.

The fulfillment of God's perfect will and promise was yet to come. When it is impossible with man, it is always possible with God. Now, well beyond childbearing years, Sarah gave birth to Isaac, the son God promised to Abraham. Isaac's seed became the Hebrew nation.

Sarah took things into her own hands, and the Arabs and Jews have been in conflict ever since.

When I read those two stories, I prayed that, by the grace of God, I **never** take things into my own hands. One disastrous mistake, I realized, can change the course of history. It put a godly fear in my heart.

*"The wise woman builds her house, But the foolish tears it down with her own hands"* (Proverbs 14:1).

Staying in my proper place as a woman has been a tremendous responsibility. The more I learned from scripture, the more important my place in the family became to me. Jim could be a leader only to the extent that the children and I learned, and were willing, to follow his authority.

*"One [a pastor] that ruleth well his own house, having his children in subjection with all gravity. (For if a man know not how to rule his own house, how shall he take care of the house of God?)"* (I Timothy 3:4,5).

*"Even so must their wives be grave, not slanderers, sober-minded, faithful in all things"* (I Timothy 3:11).

Submission isn't always an easy task. Doing what Jim asks sometimes bumps against my self-will. One of the greatest tests came about when our son Joshua was four years old.

Jim attended an annual pastors' seminar, along with about 1100 other leaders, and came home all excited. One of the topics of the day was the newly emerging home-school movement. After relating the events of the day, he enthusiastically asked, "What would you think about home-schooling Josh?"

I could tell by Jim's excitement that this was not an idle question! Many thoughts flew through my mind in the next few seconds. *I was waiting to send him to kindergarten next year! I need time for myself. What about the book I keep threatening to write?* When I composed myself internally, I calmly asked, "What do you have in mind?" I felt as though a bomb had been dropped in my lap!

"My idea is just to try teaching Josh in a casual way this year. He isn't ready for school until next year anyway. That way, we'll know if it'll work. Would you be willing to try that?" Jim answered.

*Hadn't Jim agreed that Joshua was not necessarily hyper-active, just super-active? Hadn't Josh given me some experiences that I was sure I was too old for?*

I thought about the day he found a bucket of tar  Jim was using to repair a roof. Looking out the window, I saw a black child coming down the sidewalk. It was Josh, brush in hand. He had proudly painted his jungle gym with the tar. Another time, he and our grandson Christopher picked mulberries in our yard and squeezed the juice all over their clothes and bodies. They were playing "bleeding"! Sending Josh off on the big yellow bus to kindergarten had sounded better all the time!

*Was I willing to submit to something I knew would please my husband?*  "Yes, honey, I'll try," I replied.

So many thoughts and questions were in my mind, but stronger was the admonition in scripture, *"Wives, submit yourselves unto your own husbands, as it is fit in the Lord"* (Colossians 3:18).

Josh, as a baby, seemed slow. He didn't speak clearly until he was three. I wondered if I **could** teach him. Beginning with scripture memorization, I soon saw a miracle taking place. Joshua committed long passages of scripture to memory. As we then went on to phonics, numbers, colors, and shapes, I found that he loved to learn, and I loved to teach him! Busying his mind with learning helped with some of the behavior problems. By the time he was ready to enter kindergarten, I wouldn't have let him go for anything! He was reading very well, and I saw wonderful things happening in my relationship with our youngest son.

As the years passed, we have never sent Joshua to school. Home-schooling has proven to be the best decision we have made in Joshua's behalf.

Observing Joshua's behavior, an acquaintance who worked with learning-disabled children told us that Josh would be one of her pupils if he were in a conventional classroom. She saw that his distractibility would prevent him from focusing on learning.

In recent years, we discovered that he has Attention Deficit Disorder. That knowledge explained some of his high energy level and inability to focus on anything when there was the slightest confusion around him.

God knew exactly what He was doing when he placed this child in a home with no young siblings, few distractions, and parents who would be willing to home-school him. We have been able to optimize on God's best for this son He placed in our care. Home-schooling has prepared Josh to test consistently in the 90+ percentile range on the national standardized achievement tests he takes each year.

It hasn't always been easy for me. Keeping Josh focused on the task at hand requires many hours of my time. There are still days I'd like to put him on the big yellow school bus, but it isn't even an option. The benefits far outweigh the personal costs.

Had I refused to submit to Jim's initial request to try home-schooling for a year, I would have missed a blessing for me and deprived Joshua of God's best for him.

## Chapter Six

### Acknowledging Him as Communicator

*"Now therefore go, and I will be with thy mouth, and teach thee what thou shalt say"* (Exodus 4:12).

### West Middle School, Hartford, Connecticut 1951
"SanDee is our next candidate for president of the student council," announced a teacher to the gathered student body in the auditorium. It was my turn for a campaign speech.

Shaking in every fiber of my being, I walked to the podium and proceeded to have a violent coughing spasm. I couldn't stop, as tears rolled down my cheeks. Defenseless, I stood there for several minutes trying to regain my composure. It was no use. Humiliated, I fled from the stage, ending my speaking career and bid for the presidency of my eighth-grade class. *Never again will I try to speak in front of people,* I vowed to myself.

### Kansas City, Missouri July 21, 1990
"Our testimony speaker for the evening is SanDee Stone," announced the moderator at the Gideon's International Convention. Over three thousand Gideons and their wives from several countries around the world were gathered in the large auditorium.

As I walked to the podium, I was filled with gratitude for the opportunity to share what a Gideon Bible in a Las Vegas hotel room had meant to a searching teenager. My heart was at peace, my knees didn't knock, and I delivered my message with no nervousness whatsoever.

What made the difference? I was called, by Jesus, to be a witness. I was promised in **Exodus 4:12** that He would be with me and teach me what to say. All I had to do was relax and let **Him** do what I could never do in my own strength.

### West Palm Beach, Florida 1971
My healing from cancer was the incentive I needed to launch me into sharing my testimony wherever and whenever invited. The first

invitation I received was to speak for Christian Women's Club. As I stood before a group of ladies gathered in a lovely restaurant, I was apprehensive as I recalled my eighth-grade vow never again to attempt public speaking. Now I marveled at the sudden wave of peace that flooded my soul. Speaking for 25 minutes, I was struck with how easy it was to share about Jesus. My motivation had changed - that was the difference. I wasn't standing to make a speech about how wonderful **I** was but about how wonderful **He is.** That allowed His power to work through me.

### Juno Isles, Florida 1976

"Would you teach a Bible study in my home?" a friend asked.

*Sharing my testimony is one thing,* I thought. *Teaching a Bible study is quite another. I don't know enough.* "I'll pray about it and let you know," I answered.

Seeking the Lord, I was directed to a passage of scripture in **I Corinthians 2:1-5:**

*"And I, brethren, when I came to you, came not with excellency of speech or of wisdom, declaring unto you the testimony of God. For I determined not to know any thing among you save Jesus Christ, and him crucified. And I was with you in weakness, and in fear, and in much trembling. And my speech and my preaching were not with enticing words of man's wisdom, but in demonstration of the Spirit and of power; That your faith should not stand in the wisdom of men, but in the power of God."*

*When I give my testimony, I do it in His strength. If I teach other women, He can lead me to teach those things that are real to my own heart. After all, isn't that what a witness is - telling what you have personally seen and heard?*

But the more I prayed and thought about a Bible study, the more disturbed I felt inside. The reluctance I was feeling was no longer because I doubted my ability to teach or because I didn't have the time. Something else was rumbling around in my spirit, and I needed to know what.

Praying for understanding, I finally saw what was troubling me. *Why do some women's Bible studies bear bad fruit in the lives of those attending?* I wondered. *I've seen so many women grow more knowledgeable in the scriptures and then become Pharisees - emphasizing their husband's ignorance of the Bible. In the meantime, beds go unmade, children come home from school to empty houses, dinner is late - all because Mom is at a meeting "getting spiritual."*

Putting aside a very negative attitude towards my teaching another fruitless women's Bible study, I kept my promise and asked, "Lord, what would you have me teach if I accept the invitation?"

His answer was simple. He directed me to **Titus 2:3-5:**

*"The aged women likewise, that they be in behavior as becometh holiness, not false accusers, not given to much wine, teachers of good things, That they may teach the young women to be sober-minded, to love their husbands, to love their children, To be discreet, chaste, keepers at home, good, obedient to their own husbands, that the word of God be not blasphemed."*

In this passage, I saw God's outline for women teaching women. Realizing that if I remained faithful and emphasized the things that are important to Him, I couldn't go wrong. Verse three instructed that, as an older woman, I had to first have my own life in order - hypocrites are not to teach others! Verses four and five then outlined what to teach. My goal, no matter what portion of scripture I chose to use, should have as the end result women who function more perfectly in their homes. If I were to fail to communicate that message, regardless of how wonderfully gifted I might be as a teacher, God would consider me a failure.

With direction from the Lord, peace in my heart was restored. I called my friend. "I'll teach," I said.

That Bible study went on for three years. We covered many topics - from order in the home and the women of the Bible to the commandments of Jesus. Each lesson was personally applied to how we could better perform our God-given responsibilities as wives and mothers.

One of our first projects was to make a chart depicting God's order for the home. There were no verses on the chart, just the actual photos of each woman's family members. (See drawing in chapter 5)

A favorite story of mine is about Dottie. She dutifully made her chart and posted it on her refrigerator door. That night, her husband, Pete, couldn't help noticing it and asked for an explanation. "I'm learning that my place in the family is under your authority," she shared.

Pete was shocked! What in the world had happened to his "liberated" wife? He dragged in every neighbor he could find and stood them in front of the refrigerator. "Look!" he exclaimed, "Dottie is learning her place!"

In the beginning, unsaved Pete never noticed that Jesus was on the chart above him, waiting for him to submit to His authority. All he noticed was Dottie's place under him.

Dottie expressed her submission to her husband's authority by quietly living her life in obedience to God's Word. Pete knew that only Jesus could have changed his wife so dramatically. A year later, he accepted Christ - won without a word by the behavior of his wife.

### Middletown, New York  December 8, 1987

The Christian Women's Club meeting had ended. Another opportunity to share my testimony was over, and I noticed a very excited looking lady with a warm smile waiting to talk to me. "Have you ever shared your testimony with the Gideons?" she asked. (When I speak, I always mention accepting Christ through a Gideon Bible.)

"It's funny that you should ask," was my reply. "Last summer when we were on vacation, we were staying in a motel in North Carolina. I was reading the Gideon Bible in the room, and I copied down the address of the Gideon's headquarters. Realizing that I had never thanked them for the impact their ministry had on my life, I pledged to do so. When we returned from vacation, I stuck the notebook in a dresser drawer and promptly forgot all about it."

I was too slow to act, so God sent this dear lady to remind me of my pledge. She introduced herself as Janet DeVries, wife of the New

York state Gideon president, Hank DeVries. "Would you be willing to speak for the Gideons?" Janet asked.

For many years, I had been happy to share my testimony when asked, so I answered, "Yes, it would be an honor."

Janet mentioned that she'd give my name to her husband and that she was sure my testimony would really be used by the Gideons.

It wasn't too long before Hank called, and opportunities to speak for the Gideons at Pastors' Appreciation Banquets began.

Every year, a banquet is given to honor the local pastors in each area of a state to thank them for allowing the Gideons to come into their churches. My testimony is given at such banquets to encourage both pastors and local Gideons with the effectiveness of the ministry. In addition, the Gideons host annual conventions at the state and international levels. At each of these conventions, a Pastors' Appreciation Banquet is held.

Once a year in churches, the Gideons give a report on their worldwide work, and an offering is taken. From the start, Jim and I were impressed by the Gideon ministry. Every cent collected for Bibles goes to that purpose. Operating expenses come from the pockets of the Gideon members.

We lived in New York for fifteen months after I started speaking for the Gideons. During that time, I spoke for many local area meetings as well as several state conventions. When we moved to a mountain top in Arkansas in March 1989, I lamented to Jim, "Guess that ends my speaking for anyone! No one will find us on a mountain in Arkansas!" Oh, how easy it is to try to limit a limitless God!

The month we moved to Arkansas, my testimony was published in the Gideon magazine. A caption under a picture of Jim and me mentioned that we were moving to Huntsville, Arkansas! It wasn't very long before the phone was again ringing with speaking invitations. In a little over six years, Janet DeVries' words proved to be truly prophetic! I have been privileged to share my testimony for the Gideons alone nearly a hundred times across the country.

One of the highlights of speaking for the Gideons happened in April, 1992. The Nevada-California South State Convention was to be held in Las Vegas. I answered the phone one day to a Gideon at the other end asking, "How would you like to give your testimony in Las Vegas?"

The emotions that phone call evoked are difficult to convey - excitement, awe, gratitude! How could I go back to Las Vegas and speak without dissolving in a flood of tears! "Would I like to go to Las Vegas and share my testimony? It would be the greatest thrill of my life!" I answered. *Dear Jesus,* I silently prayed, *thank you for such an honor.* The convention was held downtown, not far from the Fremont Hotel. Jim and I walked to the Fremont. As we stood in front of the Golden Nugget Casino, gazing across the street at the place where life really began 34 years ago, my heart swelled with praise to my God. I looked at the swarms of people passing by now, as I'm sure they were then, and was thrilled to think that a loving God would reach down and rescue one young Jewish girl from the pleasure-seeking crowds.

I was to speak on Friday night. That afternoon, we took another nostalgic walk to the church that had meant so much to me. The Bishops had long since gone on to be with the Lord, but standing there remembering their love brought joy and thankfulness to my heart. How I wished I could share in person all that had transpired in my life over the years. *Maybe the current pastor would like to hear my story,* I thought. The parsonage I remembered next door to the church was gone. The church itself had been enlarged, but the original building was still there as the main sanctuary. We went around to a side door marked CHURCH OFFICE. To my disappointment, the pastor wasn't in. *How can I communicate all that is in my heart anyway,* I wondered as we turned away. Jim held my hand tightly, his eyes moist as he reflected on what could have been if God hadn't intervened in our lives.

Friday evening arrived and, at last, I stood at the podium ready to speak. Again, I felt the peaceful anointing of the Holy Spirit undergirding my deep emotions. I concluded my testimony as I always did when speaking for the Gideons. "I have a debt of gratitude to one faithful Gideon who one day prayed over and placed that Bible in the room at the Fremont Hotel. I'm sure this side of Heaven, I'll never meet the man." (After all, it was 34 years ago.)

Soon after stepping down from the platform to speak to individuals who were waiting, I was approached by an elderly man with tears in his eyes. "Mrs. Stone," he began, "I was the man." Eighty-year-old Laster Arnold, a Gideon for 40 years, went on to tell me about his part in my salvation. "In 1958 when you were saved, the Fremont Hotel was fairly new. Our Gideon camp in Las Vegas had dwindled until, for three years, I was the only one left. Discouraged, I entertained the idea of leaving the ministry, but my wife Brenda talked me into signing up for another year. By the time I made the distribution of Bibles in the Fremont Hotel, another Gideon had moved into Las Vegas, and we worked together. I even have a picture taken in the lobby of the Fremont Hotel the day we dedicated and distributed the Bibles."

*"Now unto him who is able to do exceedingly abundantly above all that we ask or think, according to the power that worketh in us, Unto him be glory ... "* (Ephesians 3:20,21a).

Never did I expect to be able to personally thank the man who had provided me with the Word of God! Hugs and tears couldn't adequately express my gratitude, but I suspect that Laster knew. Later, when I sent him and Brenda a picture of our Christian family, I think they did some rejoicing of their own! Their one act of obedience has produced so much good fruit!

Laster showed me the picture that was taken over thirty years ago on the day of the Bible distribution at the Fragment Hotel. I felt I couldn't contain my delight. There, standing next to Laster in the photo, was the president of the ministerial association - Walter Bishop! How I treasure the copy I now have of that picture.

When I thought things couldn't get any better, I found that the Gideons had arranged for me to share my testimony the following Sunday morning in the same church where I had walked the aisle with Mrs. Bishop to make my first public confession of faith in Christ. *Father, you are so good to your children!*

The purpose of my speaking for the Gideons has been to encourage them. However, Jim and I have received so much personal encouragement from the wonderful friends we have made all over the country. We also have had many opportunities to share our testimony together in churches, as people have asked to hear "the rest of the story."

### North Palm Beach, Florida  February 1991

One weekend after I spoke in Florida, my Gideon host and hostess took me to the airport. Roy asked his wife, Pat, to give me a little New Testament. These are called "personal worker Testaments," used to present when witnessing about Christ.

Roy told me. "This isn't for you. It's to give away."

I thanked Roy and Pat, stuck the Testament in my purse, and wondered whom I'd meet on the plane to give it to. Nobody sat next to me all the way home, and I didn't have one conversation! That little Testament remained in my purse, and I wondered when I'd have an opportunity to share it with someone.

A week later, I flew to New York. *Lord, do you want me to witness to someone on this flight?* I prayed. Again, there was no opportunity, and the Testament remained in my purse.

This was not a trip for a speaking engagement but to be with our daughter Bonnie and her husband, Chris, for the birth of their third child. On February 13, we were blessed by the arrival of our ninth grandchild, Laura Elizabeth.

The day before I was to return home, Dee called. She, her mom, brother, and sister, had been members of the church Jim pastored when we lived in New York. "I heard you were in town and wanted you to know that my Dad is in the hospital. He hurt his back," she said.

*The Bible's for John.* The thought was loud and clear, and I immediately rejected it. *There's no way I can go to see him alone, Lord. You know what kind of man he is!*

*The Bible's for John.* More emphatic was the message, and more emphatic were my reasons not to go to the hospital. John was an unbeliever who had put his Christian wife and children through a lot of misery. We had tried to witness to him many times, but to no avail. He finally left his wife for a much younger woman. There were many unresolved hurts. How could I possibly go to see him? I had felt his wife's pain too deeply. *I know!* I reasoned, *Jim and I will be back in*

*New York soon. I'm speaking at the Pennsylvania Gideon Convention on April 2. We can go together to see John, and I'll give him the Testament.* We planned to visit Bonnie and Chris so Jim could see his new granddaughter.

That night I couldn't sleep. John was heavy on my mind. Wrestling with what I knew was right to do, I finally told the Lord that I would go to the hospital the next day.

When I walked into John's room, I was shocked to see how thin he was. He, in turn, was just plain shocked to see me back in New York.

"John," I began, "I was speaking in Florida recently for the Gideons, and a man gave me a New Testament to give away. I've carried it around for several weeks asking whom it was for. Last night, the Lord told me to give it to you." My voice quavered as I spoke, waiting for John to order me out of his room.

Instead, he started to cry. That was not the reaction I expected! "I know God sent you," he said. "I thought I was here because I had pulled something in my back. This morning, the results of the X-rays came back, and the doctor told me that I am riddled with cancer."

The Lord helped me to clearly communicate with John his need to get things right with his family and with God. I was filled with both compassion and boldness. This formerly robust, "macho" man was brought face to face with his need for a Savior, and he was listening. Using that little Testament, I showed John the "helps" in the front of the book that pointed the way to verses for every circumstance of life - fear, depression, anxiety, etc. I then reviewed the plan of salvation on a page in the back of the book. With that and an emotional prayer time together, I left John with his own thoughts. There were many things for which he needed to repent, and that was something he needed to face alone with God.

The next day I flew back to Arkansas. I heard from John's family in the weeks to come. The fact that he had fully committed his life to Christ was evidenced by his changed life. He had sought and received forgiveness from his family, and he was spending his days witnessing to all his former carousing buddies about the love of Jesus.

### Altoona, Pennsylvania  April 3, 1991

We called Bonnie from Pennsylvania to tell her when we'd be arriving in New York for a visit. "Mom, I have some terrible news for you. John died yesterday," she blurted out.

It **would** have been terrible news, had I disobeyed God and waited until Jim and I were back in New York. It would have been too late to witness to John, present him with the Testament, and see him come to faith in Jesus Christ. Instead, I now had overwhelming joy that he was in heaven.

Many times, the Lord has shown me that slow obedience is disobedience. I cried, thinking how close I had come to missing God's perfect time.

### Birmingham, Alabama  April 18, 1991

Leaving Jim and Josh visiting with Bonnie, Chris, Katy, Melissa and Laura, I flew to a Friday night Gideon meeting, planning to return to New York the next day. On the way from the airport to the motel where I'd be staying, I told my Gideon host about John. The story was still so fresh on my mind. I shared with him about the personal worker's Testament that I had received in Florida, had carried to New York, and had used to point John to Jesus. That evening after the banquet, the same Gideon who had transported me from the airport handed me another Testament. "You seem to have a good track record," he joked. "Here's another one to give away!" I placed it in my purse and wondered how long this one would stay there.

Arriving a little early at the airport the next day, I sat down in the waiting area. Glancing around, I noticed a couple sitting across the lobby. The man was wearing dark glasses and appeared to be blind. *I wonder if he's always been blind, or how he lost his sight?*

Soon, the preboarding call was given for my flight, and the woman sitting next to the blind man gently led him onto the ramp.

When I boarded the plane, I searched the overhead numbers for my seat. I was pleased to find that the blind man was sitting in the window seat, his wife was sitting in the center, and I on the aisle in the same row. This flight was destined for Atlanta, half an hour away.

*Lord, please show me a way to start a conversation about you,* I pleaded.

It wasn't long before the woman turned to me and said, "I don't know which is worse, 'terrible two's' or 'terrible teens'!"

"Why neither has to be terrible," I answered. When she asked me what I meant, I shared some of the principles we had learned in the Bible about child-rearing.

She asked if we lived in Birmingham, and I told her that I was just there overnight to share my testimony at a Gideon meeting. Suddenly, her husband leaned across her and asked, "What's your name?"

"SanDee Stone," I answered, waiting for him to continue, but he didn't. He settled back in his seat and seemed to ignore the conversation going on between his wife and me.

She asked me many questions about what I share when I speak, and I eventually told her about my salvation, healing from cancer, and Jim's getting into the ministry.

Again, the man leaned across his wife, took off his dark glasses as though to look me in the eye, and said, "Mrs. Stone, I need to ask you to pray for me."

My first impression was that he hadn't been blind long. Otherwise, why would he remove his dark glasses. *Lord, I need your wisdom.* Asking his name, I also asked what he would like me to pray for.

He went on to introduce himself as Ed, and his wife, Lois. From there, he unburdened his soul. "I've been in Birmingham at a V.A. hospital for rehabilitation. I'm in the military, and a year ago I tried to commit suicide. Obviously I failed, but my blindness is a result. As I listened to you talk to Lois, I know that the Lord can use this adversity in my life as He used your experience with cancer. Pray that I let Him."

"I'd like to give you this little New Testament," I told Ed. "It was given to me last night to give away. As you study God's word, you can be set free."

"But I can't see to read," was his reply.

Turning to Lois, I said, "You can be his eyes. Together, you can seek all the answers you both need for your family and the difficult days ahead. May I pray with you?"

**"We will be landing in Atlanta momentarily. Please secure your seatbelts, and be sure that all seats are in an upright position."**

Holding hands, we were oblivious to everything going on around us as we prayed, and Ed, with tears flowing from his blind eyes, committed his life to Jesus.

The plane had landed, and we weren't even aware of what was going on around us. Handing the little Testament to Lois, I hugged them both, and we were soon on our individual ways - Ed and Lois to South Carolina and I to New York.

The opportunities to communicate God's Word have been many and varied. When I give Him my mouth and allow Him to direct my path, He takes away any anxiety or fear.

From the time I began to share my testimony in 1971, people have approached me with numerous questions: "What about your parents? Did they ever accept you back, or did they accept Jesus? Do you have a book? I'd like to hear more of your story. How did you get from Florida to New York?"

In 1974, I began to think seriously about writing a book. For a while, I wrote earnestly. Then one day, a published author stayed in our home. She was a guest speaker for a club I belonged to. Sharing with her my desire to write, she looked at the many notes I had and was excited! We stayed up until two in the morning talking about the possibility of my writing a book.

"I have an idea," Pamela said. "Why don't you, Jim, and the children visit our summer home in North Carolina this year. You and I can work on your book, and Jim and the kids can enjoy a vacation in the mountains."

That summer, we took Pam up on her generous offer. With great expectations, we packed the car and headed for the hills! Jim and the kids had visions of cool mountain streams and a welcome respite from the Florida heat, and I welcomed the opportunity for writing help.

By that time, I had eight chapters sketched out. The theme for the book would be taken from **John 15.** *'Jesus is the vine; we are the branches. Without Him, we can do nothing.'* I'll title the book <u>Out</u> <u>on</u> <u>a</u> <u>Limb</u>; I'll show that a Christian is never really out on a limb when abiding in the vine, Jesus, as the source of strength.

Things definitely took a turn that was unexpected. Pam and her husband were having marital problems, and Jim and I spent most of the vacation counseling them. Because of problems, the atmosphere was tense and not at all conducive to writing. The few times Pam and I sat down to scrutinize my manuscript, she tried to suggest more dramatic ways to tell my anecdotes, sensationalizing what God had done. *Cecil B. Demille might do this with the Bible in Hollywood,* I thought, *but I can't do it.*

By the time the week was over, I was thoroughly confused and put the book aside. Pam had rewritten so much of it that I was disheartened. Years went by, and I could never manage to pick it up again. Then I was sure I had missed God altogether when my book title was used by the actress Shirley MacLaine.

In 1979 when we moved to New York, I thought I'd try again to write. Jim never stopped encouraging me, and I really wanted to honor his confidence. It was a lost cause though. We were restoring our old house, providing shelter, care, and counsel for a baby, two teenagers, and an adult male. Our own children Bonnie and Jeff were still at home. "Grand Central Station" is not the place to write a book, and it was put in a file cabinet again. My heart just wasn't in it.

Jim bought a new computer in Arkansas in February 1993. "Now you can write your book," he said. "The computer has a good word processor, you have the time, and my study is a quiet retreat; what do you think?"

"I think God will have to put the desire in my heart again. I have no incentive to write," was my reply.

### Nashville, Tennessee  April 1993

As soon as Jim could get my attention, he told me of an interesting conversation he had after the Pastors' Appreciation Banquet at the Tennessee State Gideon Convention. "You were busy talking when an officer from the Gideon's headquarters told me that he was sitting with a publisher from a large Christian publishing company. He mentioned thinking that you should write a book! I told him that I've been saying that for 20 years!" Jim laughed.

It was suggested that I send some things I had written to this publisher for his evaluation. In the next few weeks, I compiled and sent to him some articles I had written for a Christian magazine in New York, my testimony, and a few other things. His response gave me the guidance I needed. "Use a thematic or topical approach to issues of life, salted with your anecdotes of God's faithfulness," was his suggested format. The minute I read the letter, a teaching Jim had given on **Proverbs 3:5,6** popped into my head. He had talked about not compartmentalizing Jesus but acknowledging Him in all your ways. "That means as your realtor, your car salesman, and your provider in every area of your life," Jim had said.

At last, I was excited about writing again. Soon after receiving the letter from the publisher, a couple we didn't know very well visited our home for an overnight stay. Esther and I talked about writing. She had felt for some time that she was supposed to write, too. Remembering some sage advice I received twenty years ago, I told Esther, "Once a retired professor from the University of Connecticut tried to encourage me to write. His suggestion was to write ten or fifteen minutes a day, putting ideas on paper. He told me not to review them or try to have any semblance of order - just record data. I did that off and on for many years and have a lot of material in notebooks, journals, and on disorganized scraps of paper. Why don't we covenant together to write seriously for ten minutes a day and see what the Lord does with it?"

Esther readily agreed. I began to compile all my notes from here and there and put them in order. I now had a theme for a book, and the chapter titles would be the ways in which I acknowledge God. From no enthusiasm, I was now reluctant to stop writing at the end of ten minutes and usually wrote for long periods of time.

In early October, the phone rang and the man at the other end introduced himself saying that he was from Chattanooga. I mistakenly assumed it was about the three Gideon meetings I was scheduled for on the weekend of October 8 in that city. "No, I was wondering if you have a contract on your book?" Herman asked. "Our publishing company is interested in it."

"A contract?" I asked incredulously. "I've just started writing the book!"

By the time the conversation ended, we agreed to meet on the Saturday I was to be in Chattanooga. It definitely seemed to be God's timing.

In retrospect, I realize that one of the most essential attributes of God is that He is never in a hurry but always on time. Had I written a book when I originally planned, it would have been shallow, filled with mountaintop experiences. Had I written it a few years later, during some dark valley places in our lives, it would have sounded defeated.

The mountaintop blessings gave us a tangible basis for our faith and trust in God. They held us in times of deep testing as we walked through the valleys along our path of life. That process has taken years of walking with the Lord and will continue as long as we live. It's God's maturing program. Today I can share both mountains and valleys because I realize that each is necessary to balance my walk of faith.

*"The voice of him that crieth in the wilderness, Prepare ye the way of the Lord, make straight in the desert a highway for our God. Every valley shall be exalted, and every mountain and hill shall be made straight, and the rough places plain; and the glory of the Lord shall be revealed, and all flesh shall see it together; for the mouth of the Lord hath spoken it."* (Isaiah 40:3-5).

## Chapter Seven

## Acknowledging Him as Comforter

*"This is my comfort in my affliction: for thy word hath quickened me"* (Psalm 119:50).

"Have there ever been times when things didn't work out or when prayers weren't answered as you wished?" This question was posed during my first interview with the publisher of this book. I had just enthusiastically shared so many "happy ending" anecdotes with him.

"Yes," I replied, "and I'll be faithful to share those stories, too."

Later, as I thought about the grievous times in my life, they no longer seemed so devastating. Reviewing these once painful memories, I can honestly agree with this truth in God's Word as I record them:

*"And we know that all things work together for good to them that love God, to them who are the called according to his purpose"* (Romans 8:28).

Not just the good things, but all the circumstances of my life have worked that balance I spoke of in the previous chapter. As a Christian, I came to understand that the Bible is not a smorgasbord. I couldn't select passages and promises that I liked and pass others by. *"... In the world you shall have tribulation..."* (John 16:33). Who would choose a promise like that on purpose? However, Jesus finishes the verse with hope, *"....But be of good cheer; I have overcome the world."* He gave me His Holy Spirit to comfort and guide me through the storms of life. That makes all the difference.

Perhaps this familiar poem best says what is in my heart.

### Footprints

One night I dreamed a dream.
I was walking along the beach with my Lord.
Across the dark sky flashed scenes from my life.
For each scene, I noticed two sets
of footprints in the sand,

one belonging to me
and one to my Lord.
When the last scene of my life shot before me
I looked back at the footprints in the sand.
There was only one set of footprints.
I realized that this was at the lowest
and saddest times of my life.
This always bothered me
and I questioned the Lord
about my dilemma.
"Lord, you told me when I decided to follow You,
You would walk and talk with me all the way.
But I'm aware that during the most troublesome
times of my life there is only one set of footprints.
I just don't understand why, when I needed You most,
You leave me."
He whispered, "My precious, child,
I love you and will never leave you
never, ever, during your trials and testings.
When you saw only one set of footprints
it was then that I carried you."

Margaret Fishback Powers

He truly has been with me, carrying me through the valleys of my life. As my mountains have been leveled and valleys raised up, I've learned to trust Him as my comforter. Learning this lesson, however, was not without a great deal of pain. It meant being willing to trust Him when I couldn't understand His reasoning with my human intellect. The comfort came from acknowledging that I didn't have to. He has everything in control.

**Anne and Ron**
Sometimes imagining what God might ask me to do, I would think of pretty lofty things like going to China as a missionary. In

reality, I found that God wanted me to be a missionary right in my own neighborhood.

*Go next door and visit  Anne.*

The thought was strong, but I was in the midst of sweeping our front patio area. It was almost supper time, and I was eager to finish my task. Jim would soon be home from work, and dinner needed to be started. This was not an opportune time to visit anyone. However, relenting, I leaned my broom against the wall and headed across the yard to the house next door.

Anne and Ron were a young couple expecting their first baby any day now. Quiet and introverted, they were difficult to get to know. I was nervous about invading their privacy at dinnertime, but I was more apprehensive about disobeying the Lord.

I knocked on the door and Ron answered. He invited me into their living room, where Anne, large with child, was sitting in a comfortable chair. Her swollen feet were propped on a footstool. I could certainly empathize with Anne's discomfort, and told her so. Offering to help if they needed us and assuring them of our love, I visited a short while and left. Nothing significant was said. I wondered what that was all about as I crossed the lawn and resumed my task at hand.

The next afternoon, I was at a local hospital visiting a friend. *That looks like Ron down the corridor,* I thought. *I wonder if Anne had the baby?*

"Ron?" I called out.

Turning, a sobbing Ron ran down the hall and into my arms. Fighting to regain composure, he told me the tragic news. "Last night, Anne went into labor. Our baby, a tiny four-pound girl, was born dead. Anne is in a coma from an overwhelming toxic infection. Please help us," he cried. All I could do was stand there and cry with him. His whole life was falling apart. Sadly, he didn't know the Lord, who was the only one who could truly comfort him. But this wasn't a time for words; it was a time for tears. *"....weep with them that weep"* **(Romans 12:15b).**

The next ten days were a blur. Jim and I attended to a myriad of details for Ron. We called both sets of  parents who lived out of state, picked them up at the airport, fixed meals, and helped Ron with the sad task of arranging for the baby's funeral. We were there to pray and weep with all of them.

Anne remained in a coma. She never regained consciousness, and at the end of ten days, she died. Her body couldn't overcome the infection.

When I had offered to help the day I visited Anne and Ron, I couldn't have imagined the consequences. Ron asked if Jim and I would conduct the funeral service for both Anne and their baby girl. We had to rely fully on the strength of the Lord. He promised that He would be our comfort as we walked through the valley of death.

Not even beginning to understand why God allowed such a tragedy, the lesson I learned was the importance of being available for God's timing and obedient to His schedule. We were to be Jesus' loving hands, feet, arms and heart to a family in need, and we had the peace that obedience affords.

### Patti

"Patti has cancer," was the alarming report sounded throughout the academy community. Patti, a former graduate, was a much loved young lady - exemplary in her life as a Christian witness. A suspicious mole turned out to be a deadly melanoma, and Patti was given no hope.

When I heard the news, I was more than distressed. Having taught Home Economics at the academy for a while, Patti was one of my favorite pupils and was a fellow classmate and friend of our daughter Loryn. I didn't personally know her family and wondered if there was anything I could, or should, do. I prayed, "Lord, you healed me of cancer. I know you can heal Patti. Please let me know if I'm to talk to her or her family."

Not many days passed before Patti's mother called. Introducing herself, she then said, "We were told that you were healed of cancer. Could you visit Patti and share your testimony with us?"

By her calling, I assumed that God was indeed going to heal Patti. With confidence and joy, I visited her many times in the weeks to come. I shared my testimony as I was asked to do. I shared books and tapes that had inspired me during my illness. Most important of all, I shared my heart as we prayed together.

When I learned that her mother was a widow, I was even more assured of Patti's healing. She was an ideal Christian daughter. Couldn't we claim the following promise in God's Word?

*"Children, obey your parents in the Lord; for this is right. Honor your father and mother (which is the first commandment with promise), That it may be well with thee, and thou mayest live long on the earth"* **(Ephesians 6:1-3).**

By faith, I claimed this scripture for Patti. She did obey and honor her mother. It would be well with her, and she'd live a long life.

Patti gradually began to improve. Encouragement ran high! We were seeing the miracle so many had hoped and prayed for! Then, with absolutely no warning, Patti had a seizure and died.

I was confused, bewildered, and most of all, angry with God. "How could you let her die? Why did you let me go to see her and give her a false sense of security? Why did you give us hope then take her away? Why? Why? Why?" I railed. "I'll never tell anyone else about my healing!"

The anger and tears finally were spent in utter exhaustion, and I lay down across the bed. Sleep wouldn't come. God patiently waited for my temper tantrum to cease. When I finally was quiet, I heard a still, small voice whisper to my troubled spirit, *Don't "why" me, worship me.*

That had to be one of the most profound lessons I ever learned. Trusting God means recognizing that He is sovereign. He doesn't have to give me clear understanding in every situation. I can stamp my feet like a petulant child and that won't change God's sovereignty one bit. My obligation as His follower is to worship and obey Him. The results are His. He sees the beginning and end of every life. If allowed, He can comfort in the darkest hour.

Repenting of my folly, I rededicated myself to trusting Him, even in the incomprehensible times.

Patti's funeral was a celebration of joy. She was safe in the arms of Jesus. Tears flowed as the song "It Is Well With My Soul" was sung.

They weren't bitter tears but tears of cleansing. *Lord, I will worship you. It is well with my soul.*

### Orlando

In August 1976, returning from a lengthy family vacation, Jim and I felt a strange restlessness when we reentered Florida. "It's odd, but I feel as though this is no longer going to be our home," Jim confessed.

There arose a desire within both of us to leave Florida, and the more we prayed about it, that seemed to be God's message to us. *You'll be leaving Florida.*

We began to pray specifically for the Lord to show us how, when, and where to move. In November, the day after Tim's fall from the tree, Jim received a phone call from a former teacher at the academy where he was employed. Bob had since moved to Orlando to start another Christian school. He told Jim, "I met a man here in Orlando who is helping to convert a secular vocational-technical college into a Christian school. It'll be the first two-year Christian vo-tech school in the country. Some of the non-Christian staff has to be replaced, and there is a need for someone to head up the computer department. I immediately thought of you. I spoke to the president of the school, and he'd like you to call if you're interested."

For four days, the phone number sat on his desk while Jim prayed. *I felt we were going to be leaving,* he thought. *Maybe this is it! Maybe God meant leave the area, not the state.*

During that time, we ran through a wide spectrum of thoughts and emotions. On one hand, we wondered if we were willing to leave our friends, families, the academy, the church, and our home to go to a big city like Orlando? On the other hand, we felt excited and pretty confident that we would be leaving.

Jim called and sent the resume they requested. In a few days, he was asked to come to Orlando for an interview. He was hired, contingent on his release from his contract at the academy. The release was granted and Jim left for Orlando.

We placed our house on the market, assuming it would sell quickly so that our family could be reunited. In the meantime, Bob invited Jim to stay in their Orlando home during the week. Every Friday night, he made the three-hour trip to Lake Park to be with us. During that time, Jim continued to pastor the church meeting in our home. Every Sunday evening, he left again for the lonely drive back to Orlando.

One unusually cold weekend in January, I drove to Orlando to house-hunt with Jim. Even then, I desired a two-story house with a fireplace. We looked at several places until we found the house of my dreams. It was on a city street with no yard to speak of, but it had two stories and a fireplace. The house was charming! The living room furniture was cozily grouped around a brick fireplace complete with a blazing fire. An attractive scatter rug on a polished hardwood floor completed the picture. Off to the side of the living room was a sunroom with banks of windows. The sun streamed in on white wicker furniture padded with floral print chintz cushions. A basket of yarn balls in matching colors sat on the floor. The kitchen and sunny breakfast nook would invite anyone to linger over a cup of morning coffee. Yes, this had to be the perfect house!

I was confident that now our house would sell, and soon we'd be settled into this wonderful replacement. It didn't. As a matter of fact, the house in Orlando sold quickly - to someone else. Heartbroken, I wondered if we'd ever be together again. I was also sure we'd never find a house as nice as the one we just lost.

Four months passed. They were the most discouraging four months we had ever experienced. Jim's job turned out to be extremely disappointing. Instead of holding true to the conversion from secular to Christian, the college board began to compromise their standards in order to retain students. Money became the central issue, rather than pleasing God. The strain of trying to sell the house, run our household all week on my own, continue to sew for customers, and care for the children was telling on me.

Then, it was over. Jim, no longer able to handle the unrighteous demands at the school, resigned and came home. With that decision, we continued in a valley for the next three years. Thankful now that our house didn't sell, we found ourselves completely bewildered about what had gone wrong. We **thought** we were in God's will.

God never stopped meeting our needs during those three years. The church continued to meet in our home, and Jim was able to find odd jobs to supplement our income. Business went on as usual, but there was a leanness in our soul. We knew something wasn't right, but we couldn't seem to figure out what it was.

Then we attended a meeting that changed our lives. We don't remember the speaker or even the gist of the message, but we both heard one line, loud and clear. "We must not presume on God. When He tells us to do something, we must hear and do **exactly** what He says - no more, and no less."

We left the meeting and sat in the car in deep repentance and gratitude. God had never abandoned us during those three years. He knew we weren't being rebellious when Jim accepted the job in Orlando, but this was a lesson He had to teach us in an emphatic way. We finally saw what we had done wrong. God had told us we'd be leaving <u>Florida</u>, not <u>the area</u>. Our rationalizing took us to Orlando and out of the perfect will of God for our lives. It took three years to get us back on the path of life He had chosen for us. The lesson was well learned, and we were comforted as we thought about what could have happened if we had sold our house and moved to Orlando out of His will.

Things happened with dizzying speed from that point forward. In a matter of months, with no effort on our part, our house was sold, and we were on our way out of Florida, to New York, and back into the will of God.

### Loryn

"My advice is to not let your daughter and grandsons come home from Florida. Her husband is potentially dangerous. They're safer where they are." This was the response from a Christian psychologist who had been seeing our son-in-law Kyle for some time. Jim called him this New Year's Day, frantic for help.

A week before, Loryn and her two children had been sent to Florida as a supposed Christmas gift from her husband. She had felt uncomfortable about leaving, and I'll long remember her conversation with me.

"Mom, I think maybe he's doing better," Loryn said, "but I don't feel right about going away."

"Maybe Grandma and Grandpa need some encouragement. They haven't been well. Seeing Christopher and Isaak may be just the medicine they need. Be gracious about the gift and go," was my response. I drove them to the airport the day after Christmas. This was going to be a two-week vacation with my parents. How could I have possibly known that I was sending my beloved first-born and only grandchildren away from us for a long, long time?

Loryn, at sixteen years of age, graduated with honors from the Christian academy. She had committed herself to not dating during high school, content to wait for God's choice in a husband for her. School and church functions were attended with groups of young people or with a boy friend (as opposed to a boyfriend). Entering college, we had no qualms about sending this daughter of ours to Minneapolis to school just before her seventeenth birthday. God had given her to us, and we were giving her back to Him for His service. She was steadfast in her walk with Him.

Bethany Fellowship Missionary Training Center had strict dating standards. Expecting their students to put Jesus first, official permission to date was forestalled until the end of their freshman year.

Loryn wasn't in school very many weeks before a young man in her class began to pay attention to her. He was older than most of the freshman because he had already been to a secular college. Now he felt called to Christian service and had entered Bethany as a freshman.

The relationship was kept at arm's length because of the school rules, and we appreciated this protection for our daughter. The day finally arrived when dating was a possibility, and Kyle soon asked Loryn to go out with him. Her reply was, "I won't date until you have my dad's approval."

This began a relationship through letters and phone calls between Jim and Kyle. We determined that this slow process of familiarization was a wonderful test of his sincerity, and he was passing it with flying colors. He even arranged to come to Florida to spend a week's vacation with us. We scrutinized this fellow as best we could and we liked him. He was polite, seemed to adore Loryn, and his conversation reflected a desire to grow spiritually. Except for some youthful immaturity, he met our approval. We gave permission for them to date, knowing that even dating came under strict guidelines at school.

After a year of dating, Kyle asked permission to marry our daughter. Permission granted, the wedding was set for just before they began their senior year.

Another test of the relationship was yet to come. All students, during their junior year, are assigned a place of internship to practice what they've learned. Loryn went to New York to work at the Walter Hoving Home, and Kyle was sent to Puerto Rico. They would be apart for almost a year.

The relationship withstood the test of separation, and soon the wedding plans were in full progress. The summer was brimming with the joyful activities of shopping, sewing, writing invitations, and attending bridal showers.

The ceremony was held on the grounds of the academy that had been such an important part of our lives. Chairs were placed in a grove of trees near a sparkling little lake. Friends and family eagerly waited for the ceremony to begin.

Loryn, her arm entwined in my dad's, started down the grassy aisle, as Jim, standing under the *chupa,* valiantly sang with quavering voice, "Is this the little girl I carried..." ("Sunrise, Sunset" from <u>Fiddler on the Roof</u>)

My parents, who wouldn't attend our wedding, were willing to take part in the wedding of their first grandchild, and Loryn wanted to honor them. The *chupa,* or canopy, is used in a Jewish wedding to represent God's covering. The bride and groom stood underneath it as Jim performed the ceremony. It was a meaningful day, and our expectations for this couple were high.

Soon they returned to Bethany for their senior year. After graduation, they headed for New York, where we now lived, to be part of our church family. Plans were set in motion to one day start a

Christian placement service for children. We were so happy for Loryn. She had always loved children, and wanted to work with them. Before long, through adoption, our first grandson, Christopher, joined the family.

Storm clouds were gathering on the horizon, and we were blinded to the warning signs. What started out as the fairy-tale wedding of Loryn's dreams soon soured into her worst nightmare.

Kyle was caught in the despicable act of voyeurism by the father of a young girl in our church. Assuring the father that he'd never done such a thing before, Kyle used all the right words in appealing to this man's Christian conscience, and forgiveness was granted.

Not realizing that this had been a problem for years, Jim advised Loryn to forgive and work through this very difficult time. Then it happened again. We learned later that it had happened many times before, but this time, Kyle was caught by someone who came to Jim. This man, not being aware of any other episodes, was duped by the same empty words of "this is the first time."

Jim saw that Kyle was not responding to his counsel. The father in Jim was sickened by what was happening to his daughter; the pastor in him wanted to believe Kyle's sincerity. Jim offered to send him to a Christian psychologist in a nearby town. He readily accepted the offer, and counseling sessions were arranged.

Loryn, standing by her husband, hoped for his complete healing, and the counseling sessions seemed to be working. Their relationship was less strained, and Loryn became pregnant.

Now the nightmare seemed to never end. Planning an act of violence against a girl he was stalking at a convenience store, Kyle sent Loryn and the children to Florida to get them out of the way. New Year's Eve was the night chosen, but nothing happened. Scared away, he instead confessed his thwarted plans to an elder in our church, who regretfully came to Jim with the dreadful news.

The next morning, Jim called the psychologist, and we shuddered as he told us the possible consequences of this problem, unchecked. "Sooner or later, it goes from fantasy to actual violence," we were warned. Again the doctor emphasized, "Do not let Loryn come back yet." He casually mentioned in the conversation that he hadn't seen our son-in-law for some time. We realized then how much we had been deceived. Jim had faithfully handed him the payment each week, believing that it was being used to pay the doctor.

If ever I needed the comfort of the Holy Spirit and the Lord's ability to forgive, it was now. Every natural human emotion screamed out for vengeance, but I knew better. Thankful for the Word of God, I chose to forgive and leave Kyle to the Lord.

*"Vengeance is mine; I will repay, saith the Lord"* **(Romans 12:19).**

*"..If you forgive not men their trespasses, neither will your Father forgive your trespasses"* **(Matthew 6:15).**

Loryn and the boys were safe from harm. I was confident that Jim would handle this problem with righteousness.

*"Thou wilt keep him in perfect peace, whose mind is stayed on thee, because he trusteth in thee"* **(Isaiah 26:3).**

*Lord, I know you know how much I'm hurting for my child. You hurt while watching your Son suffer. Thank you for the comfort of your peace. Please comfort Loryn when I tell her.*

Calling Loryn at my parents was a difficult thing to do, but we really had no choice. The news was difficult for her to hear but not shocking. She had been through so much more than we realized in the last few years.

My parents had a small, one-bedroom apartment. It was fine for a short visit, but this could be an extended stay. Our suggestion was for Loryn and the boys to go to Clearwater, Florida, and stay with my brother who had a vacant cottage on his property. Not knowing what else to do, Loryn agreed. I spoke with my brother, and he was willing to help.

The next Sunday in church, Jim painfully stood before the congregation and disfellowshipped Kyle, according to **I Corinthians 5.** By withholding fellowship, there was the hope of shame, repentance, and restored fellowship. We prayed that it would work.

Unfortunately, the announcement opened a Pandora's box. The few isolated incidents that Jim was aware of became only the tip of the iceberg. Several others came forward to relate their story. In each case, they had remained silent, having been told it was 'the first time.'

*"For nothing is secret, that shall not be made manifest; neither any thing hidden, that shall not be known and come to light"* **(Luke 8:17).**

My greatest fear was that Loryn would turn her back on us, or worse, on the Lord. After all, hadn't she done everything right? She remained pure for marriage and submitted to her dad's authority before even dating. We had certainly given her our blessing.

My fear was not realized. In the early days, Loryn's only reaction was to want to lash out and get an immediate divorce. Even in this, she listened to her dad, who advised her to stand in the place of righteousness and take no action. "God will vindicate you," Jim encouraged.

The weeks turned into months, and Loryn continued to live in the cottage. It looked as though there was no solution in sight. Since she wasn't receiving any support, she was forced to look for a job. She soon found one as a counselor for a secular drug and alcohol program.

None of us expected the next action. Her husband, who was passive by nature, had her served with divorce papers. She agreed to the divorce on one condition. To protect the children, Loryn asked that he have limited supervised visitation rights with the children. Accepting this condition, the divorce was final in a short time.

One day I was reading in the Bible about Samson **(Judges 13-16).** It seemed that the Lord used this story to explain how Kyle could choose sin and lose his family. Samson was a young man chosen by God before his birth. God had great plans for him. He was to be used to begin to deliver the Israelites out of the hands of the Philistines. But Samson disregarded the instructions of purity that God had set for his people and gave in to his fleshly desires. He lost his supernatural strength and was captured by the enemy. He died a horrible death. Three thousand Philistines died with him, and Samson accomplished more by his death than he ever did with his life. That was not God's intent. Neither was it God's intent for Kyle to lose his family. He gave him a godly wife, a forgiving church, and our family who loved him. God had a wonderful plan for Kyle's life, but he chose to walk away from it. I fully came to realize the deceitfulness of sin through Samson and Kyle.

Loryn never left Florida. In one phone conversation she mournfully told me, "All I wanted out of life was to be a wife and mother. Someday I'll have a family you and Dad can be proud of."

*"And I will restore to you the years that the locust hath eaten...... And ye shall eat in plenty, and be satisfied, and praise the name of the Lord, your God, who hath dealt wondrously with you; and my people shall never be ashamed"* (Joel 2:25a,26).

Today, Loryn does have a family we can be proud of. In time, the Lord healed her wounded heart and restored happiness for those years of pain. Working as a counselor has continued to give her an outlet to help other hurting people. She is now married to Thad, a pastor and counselor. His love and patient understanding have been a blessing. He was able to adopt Christopher and Isaak so that the past could be put solidly behind them. Today their household is filled with the happy noises of children. Micah, Amy and Jacob have been added to their family circle. Busy home-schooling the children, counseling women, and foster parenting, Loryn's joy is complete.

### Mom Stone

Mom returned from a trip to Israel a totally different person, and it wasn't because she was thrilled to have walked where Jesus walked. That was the reaction we expected. Instead, she flaunted a diamond and emerald ring purchased by a total stranger. She kicked up her heels like a giddy schoolgirl, telling us about the wonderful man she had met on the tour. Being bowled over by a feather would have been too mild a term to explain how we felt.

Dad Stone had passed away three years before, and Mom went on quietly living out her faith in Jesus. She had been the greatest influence in my life as a young believer.

When she had an opportunity to go to Israel with a church group, we encouraged her to participate. We were certain it would be a deep spiritual blessing for her, and we were thrilled when she decided to go.

Now she was home, and all we heard about was Peter. The trip to Israel seemed to pale in significance. Peter was a widower, ten years older than Mom. He lived on the west coast of Florida, had a big house, and was lonely. Traveling together on the church tour, Mom was swept off her feet by the attention Peter gave her and the gifts he bought her.

We should have seen the warning signs, but we were too bewildered to consider the absolute abnormality of her behavior.

Nothing anyone could say could prevent Mom from marrying Peter within months of coming back home. Not knowing what else to do, we wished them well and hoped for the best. He was a nice enough man but was from an entirely different, European culture. We saw a man who wanted someone to take care of him.

Mom had visions of entertaining in his spacious home. Dad Stone had never been very sociable, and this was something she longed for. Peter was already established in a large church, and Mom was convinced that they'd be very active in the seniors' group.

We were frightened for her. Peter was obviously not the sociable type. A quiet man, he seemed to be very set in his reclusive pattern of life. At seventy-five years old, he would hardly become the social butterfly.

Living across the state from us meant infrequent visits. Then we moved to New York and had to rely totally on letters and phone calls.

Mom began occasionally forgetting to acknowledge one of our birthdays - unheard of for her. Then she sent Jim a card meant for his brother Tom. Next, she sent us two cards for the same anniversary. Fear began to creep into our hearts.

Peter, upset, complained to Jim's brother, "Pat is accusing me of taking her money. I wouldn't do that. I have enough of my own."

Our initial thought was, depression. Probably things hadn't worked as Mom hoped and she was lonely, away from the family. Perhaps she was too embarrassed to confide in the family. Then again, maybe she was taking improper dosages of her blood pressure and other medication.

The family encouraged Peter to take Mom to a doctor. *Something was terribly wrong.* He wouldn't hear of it. "I can take care of Patti," he retorted.

Mom's accusations toward Peter worsened. Finally, his feelings hurt and not able to understand her strange behavior, he called Jim's brother. "Come get Patti. I don't want her anymore." All the time he was refusing to get medical help.

We felt heartsick. We suggested bringing her to New York where we could take her to a doctor. We were sure that our loving care and prayer would restore her to a sound mind. If her medication needed adjusting, we'd take care of that detail. She'd be her old self in no time!

When Mom was brought to our home, she was so much worse than we could have imagined. Where did the dear lady who loved the Lord and loved life to its fullest disappear? *What had Peter done to break her spirit?* I wondered.

Sitting in the consultation room, we listened to the doctor's evaluation of Mom's condition. "Your mother has Altzheimer's disease," he said. "She will probably continue to worsen to the point that you can't care for her at home. There is no cure. I predict that she may live another two years."

For me, it was like caring for a total stranger. The Mom we knew was lost in the fog of an irrational mind. When I finally accepted the fact that she wasn't caring for her personal hygiene, I had to take over. It became a daily battle of wills. "Mom, you can't wear three sets of underwear. Let me help you dress. Mom, it's time to wash your hair." All these daily routines were met with ironclad resistance. I loved her and considered it a privilege to care for her. Why did she resist me so?

We prayed. Oh, how we prayed, but Mom continued to worsen. She couldn't be left alone for a minute without getting into things that could harm her or annoy us. She hid everything small enough to squirrel away in vases, closet tops, books, and pockets. House keys, money, buttons off her clothing, mail - all began to disappear.

One day a work crew was working on road repairs in front of our house. Mom sneaked out and appealed to one of the men, "Help me.

I'm being held captive here." Fortunately, he questioned her sanity and returned her safely to our door. We lived in constant concern that she'd get out and lost or be hit by a car.

When she referred to me in speaking to Jim, I was reduced to "that woman you live with." She no longer knew me, and soon she didn't recognize Jim as her son.

I was comforted by the fact that I could care for her physical needs. The Lord was giving me strength on a daily basis.

One winter night, I went grocery shopping. I had to go at a time I could leave Mom safely in bed, under Jim's supervision. I was so tired. After shopping, I was surprised to find that it had been snowing the whole time I was in the store. While cautiously wending my way home on the slippery street, a car suddenly ran a stop sign at a side street and turned right in front of me. I jammed on the brakes. Skidding, I slammed into a curb. The car almost flipped but righted itself as my head hit the window, hard. I was facing the wrong way on the street when I came to my senses. Afraid that I'd now be hit head on, I managed to pull into a gas station on the opposite corner. *Jesus, help me not to pass out.*

My head was pounding as I struggled out of the car and into the warmth of the station. "Can you help me," I pleaded. "I just had an accident."

"There's the phone, lady," was the tough looking attendant's uncharitable reply, as he pointed to the pay phone on the wall. Tears filled my eyes. I didn't know how long I could remain conscious. *I can't call Jim. He can't leave Mom and Josh alone. No one else is home,* I thought. Gratefully, I remembered a family in the church who lived nearby. "Fred, this is SanDee. I just had an accident. Can you help me?"

I was never more thankful for a compassionate Christian friend. Fred was there in minutes and drove me home in his car. Ours couldn't be driven. Taking one look at me and my swollen face, Jim rushed me to the hospital. By now, Bonnie was home and could care for Mom and Josh.

As I lay there in the emergency room, I hoped that I was hurt badly enough to stay in the hospital. My exhaustion was overwhelming.

X-rays were taken, and what should have been good news, wasn't. The attending physician cheerfully exclaimed, "You can go home, Mrs. Stone. There's no concussion or broken bones - just bruises."

The next morning, I looked like a raccoon. Both eyes were rimmed in black and blue, and my head pounded whenever I bent over. Mom, incapable of understanding my predicament, seemed to delight in tormenting me. As I bent to help her with her shoes, she tossed them under the bed, out of reach.

That night, Jim called his brother. "We need to put Mom in a nursing home for a while," he said, explaining about my accident and my worn out condition.

Mom's four children deliberated on the best situation for her future care and mutually decided that a permanent nursing home in Florida would be a better option. One of her sons found a lovely nursing home, came to get her, and placed her there. I could never have made that decision. It was hard enough to release the decision to her own children. I felt so responsible.

"Jim," I asked in tears, "What about the scripture that says we're worse than an unbeliever if we don't care for Mom?" *"But if any provide not for his own, and specially those of his own house, he hath denied the faith, and is worse than an infidel"* **(I Timothy 5:8).**

Jim's answer gave me the comfort I needed, and set me free from the burden I was carrying. "We **are** providing for Mom," he said. "Now that she doesn't even know who we are, I feel released to place her in a nursing home. You're only one person - they'll be able to give her a fresh nurse each shift, round-the-clock. Under the circumstances, her care will actually be better there than here. Besides, you've given all of yourself you can give, and the family needs you, too."

Within a year, Mom went to be with the Lord.

### Daddy

Through the years, my greatest fear has been how I could live through losing one of my parents. Death, as inevitable as life, was something I would one day have to face. Knowing that they had continued to reject Christ was a source of deep grief to me.

Jim promised my folks that he'd drive to Florida and take them back to Arkansas as soon as our house was complete in 1990. My mom, being very afraid of flying, was eager to take him up on the offer. True to Jim's word, we set off for Florida as soon as the weather turned warm in May.

One night, as I was praying for my parents, I felt the Lord say, *This will be the last chance you'll have with your parents.* I didn't know what that meant. Both Mom and Dad had their minor physical ailments, usual for their advancing years, but they were in relatively good health. Daddy had recuperated nicely from a stroke. My mother's loving and diligent therapy had him walking, talking, and functioning almost as good as new. The clean Ozark mountain air would surely do them a world of good.

We went to Florida and besides Mom and Dad, Christopher and Isaak also returned to spend the summer. We had a full and busy household.

It was a wonderful summer. Mom and Dad enjoyed sitting on the front porch of our mountain top log home every evening, listening to the racket of the cicadas. They marveled at the hues of gold and red in the sky as the sun slowly set in the west. Daddy was especially enchanted by the tiny hummingbirds that buzzed around the feeder placed close to his rocking chair. Joshua, Christopher, and Isaak put on plays for us in the front yard. It was the perfect setting for Davy Crockett and Daniel Boone!

Mom and I took long walks down the mountain, and saw wonders such as a mama skunk with her furry babies tumbling after her, and white-tailed deer romping in the meadows along the way. Mom was so tired from the long months of caring for Dad after his stroke, and she loved being here for some rest and recuperation. Our son Tim, his wife, Karen, and baby, Nathanael, live in nearby Summers, Arkansas. They were a source of blessing to my folks during our several visits with them.

In August, my parents celebrated their fifty-fifth wedding anniversary, and my brother and sister-in-law came from Florida to help us celebrate. In a few days, they would take the folks back home.

*Thank you, Lord, for such a good summer. If we really never have this opportunity again, I'm grateful for what you've allowed us to have now.*

In my heart was still that nagging fear. *They don't know you, Lord.*

Soon after arriving home, Dad went for a checkup. Not feeling well, he was run through a battery of tests. When the tests were completed, he was diagnosed with lung and bone cancer. Chemotherapy was decided against because of his age and condition.

Grateful for a Gideon trip to Florida in January 1991, I was able to celebrate Daddy's eightieth birthday with him. Toward the end of March, I flew down to spend a few more days. By this time, Daddy was very weak and no longer able to walk. How I yearned to speak to him alone about his need for the Lord. I had never had that chance. Mom was always there, stifling any opportunity. Then one day she had to run to the store, and I seized the time. It was close to Passover. *Maybe I can use that holiday as a springboard,* I thought.

My heart was pounding and my mouth was dry. It was ridiculous, but I was scared to death. This might be my only chance, and I didn't want to lose it. I waited patiently until his favorite game show on TV ended, and I plunged in. "Daddy, I need to talk to you. I want you to know what it takes to go to heaven. I so want you there."

"Go on, daughter," he replied passively.

"I know you're not religious, Daddy, but you do know about the Passover lamb. When the lamb's blood was shed and applied to the door posts of the houses, the death angel passed over. Daddy, Jesus is our Passover lamb. He died, and His blood was shed for your sins. By applying that blood to your heart, you can have forgiveness and eternal life in heaven."

There was a hush. My eyes were so brimming with unshed tears that I couldn't see.

"I don't know what to say to you," was my daddy's tender reply.

"It's Him you need to talk to, not me," I answered, as the door flung open and Mom rushed breathlessly in. That ended the special moment, but I thanked God for it.

I was able to see my dad one more time, several weeks before he died. His very last words to me were whispered. He was bedridden and so weak. "You don't have to worry about me. I'm okay," he said.

In my heart, I could praise God at his funeral, instead of suffering the agony I expected. That whispered confession was God's gift of comfort to me. Whatever Daddy meant or understood, the Lord left me with hope.

## Chapter Eight

## Acknowledging Him as Defender

*"But let all those that put their trust in thee rejoice: let them ever shout for joy, because thou defendest them ... "* (Psalm 5:11a).

### West Palm Beach, Florida 1974

The phone, ringing rudely, interrupted my early morning reverie. Jim and the children had left for school, and I was enjoying my few minutes of solitude before busying myself at the sewing machine. Today promised to be a busy one. I needed to finish a dressmaking order and get to the hospital to check on my neighbor Anne.

I answered the phone with a somewhat curt, "Hello."

The man on the other end told me his name and then explained, "I'm with the FBI. There has been a bomb threat at the academy this morning, and we need you to come down immediately for questioning."

My hand shook as I held the phone. "Could you please explain?" I feebly asked.

"We need to know about the threatening letters you've been receiving," was his reply. "I'll explain more when you get here."

Now, more annoyed than anything, I drove fifteen miles on the busy interstate to the school. Fuming, I thought, *Threatening letters; what threatening letters? I haven't been receiving any threatening letters! I'm already involved in a life and death drama. My neighbor Anne is in a coma; her baby died. All my time and energy are devoted to her. I don't have time for nonsense. I need time to sew today, or I'll lose my favorite customer.*

*"Let the peace of God rule in your heart ... "* (Colossians 3:15a).

*Thank you for reminding me, Lord. I'm fretting and worrying and not taking time to allow you to rule in my heart.* On the rest of the trip, I prayed and calmed my troubled spirit.

As I prayed, I contemplated what the man on the phone had said about threatening letters. Then my memory was jogged to an isolated incident that happened several weeks before. Twice a week, I taught at the academy. One day when I arrived at school, I checked for messages in my open cubbyhole in the office hallway. There was a strange note:

"Mrs. Stone,
     Thought you'd keep things told to you between the teller, yourself, and God. You ain't doin' too good a job. Better change fast or you'll be speakin' to us ...

                                        Good luck,
                                        Experienced workers"

At the time, I had been dealing with two rebellious students and dismissed the note as foolishness. I had given it to Jim and that was that. Or was it? But there was only **one** note.

When I reached the school campus, Jim was waiting to meet me. "What in the world is going on?" I demanded.

"Maybe I shouldn't have shielded you from the other notes," Jim began, "but I thought this might have been a way for Satan to divert your attention and prayers from Anne and Ron. Please forgive me. Let's go into Mr. Landers' office. The others are waiting for us."

We hurried across campus to the president's office. Confused and dazed, I numbly followed Jim. Nothing made any sense, and my mind was filled with a torrent of unanswered questions.

When we entered the office, a grim-faced Mr. Landers, the school president, sat behind his desk. Another man whom I didn't recognize sat next to the desk. Spread in front of them was an assortment of notes typed on plain 8 1/2 by 11 paper. At a glance, they looked much like the note I had received a few weeks before.

Mr. Landers introduced me to the man from the FBI. He was the same one who had called me at home an hour before. "Jim and SanDee, please sit down," he invited. Once we were seated, he turned to address me. "SanDee, your husband has been confiscating notes from your cubbyhole in the hallway for weeks, while he and Mr. Landers have tried to get to the bottom of the problem. They thought it unnecessary to involve and upset you if it was just a childish prank. However, as the teachers arrived for work this morning, the problem became more complex. This was found on the floor in front of the cubbyholes."

With that, he handed me an envelope.

Typed on the front were these words:

Open by 9:45 A.M. for best results

The note inside unleashed one of the most bizarre episodes in my life. It read as follows:

"To The Academy,

A bomb will be planted in one of your classrooms by 9:45 this morning. It will be set to go off at exactly 10:00, 15 minutes later.

There have been many bomb threats in the state of Florida. Fifty percent have turned out to be false alarms, but don't forget the other 50 percent. We'll leave that up to you.

L.E.W.

One more thing: to find out about L.E.W. (Lucifer's Experienced Workers) speak to Mrs. Stone. She has been receiving some notes from us lately and a recent one tells of our organization."

The FBI man went on to explain. "A bomb threat cannot be taken lightly. Mr. Landers did the right thing by calling us. After all, there are over a thousand students and staff here. The school was evacuated, and the bomb squad did a thorough search. Fortunately, nothing was found. Is there anything you can remember that may shed light on the situation?"

Dumbfounded, I sat there trying to imagine what kind of warped mind would do such a thing.

Mr. Landers handed me the rest of the notes addressed to me. There might not have been a physical bomb at the academy that day, but the attack I felt was as painful. As I read the notes, I wondered, *Were these written by a student or an adult?*

One of the notes said, "Due to the dismissal of two of our L.E.W. members, the notes will be written by one of our more experienced workers who has been with the L.E.W. since '55."

*Dismissed?* If that was a clue, I didn't like the conclusions my mind was drawing. Recently a teacher had been fired and a student expelled because of an incident in which I had been involved.

Although I had originally been hired as a part-time Home Economics teacher, my assignment was temporarily changed. At the end of the previous school year, the principal asked, "How would you like to take all the seventh and eighth grade girls for one year and teach them what the Bible has to say about a girl's place in the world?"

*What a challenge,* I thought. *What an opportunity. With the Women's Liberation Movement growing at an alarming rate, this class will give me a chance to teach young minds while they are pliable.* Or so I thought!

All that summer, I developed a curriculum for this special class. I called it "Investing in Good Living." As I searched the Bible for God's point of view concerning women, I wished I could have had an opportunity at twelve or thirteen to learn the truth that these girls would be taught this next year. *God has such a beautiful, protected place for girls,* I reflected. I could hardly wait for the school year to begin!

The course would cover every aspect of a girl's life. Since teenagers are vitally interested in their appearance, we would start there. We would then continue through other topics such as their place in the family, dating, and even, with the permission of their parents, explore the "facts of life" from God's perspective.

Unfortunately, the class wasn't presented properly. The girls were told that they would **have** to take the class, and rumors flew as to the content. It took months to overcome a negative beginning. In time, there was a genuine interest in the class, sparking lively dialogue. There were still a few diehard nonparticipants, but that might be expected in any classroom situation. I was just naive enough to be totally unprepared for it in a Christian school. The majority of the students were won over by prayer and love, and they were beginning to look at themselves from God's point of view. To many, the revelation was exciting.

By April, a real closeness had developed. It was time to explore openly and honestly their sexual development as part of God's plan. Each girl's parents were given an outline of this phase of the curriculum, and all approved their daughter's participation in the class. Many of the girls asked thought-provoking questions. Even the former nonparticipants joined in. The problems began to surface when two thirteen-year-olds asked questions that made me wonder what they had been exposed to on TV or in reading material. Worse yet, I wondered what they actually were doing themselves.

I couldn't answer them publicly because of the nature of their questions. I finally decided to interview them individually in the privacy of an office.

"Carol, I'm a bit concerned about some of your questions in class," I began. "You seem to be concerned about pregnancy and other issues that shouldn't concern you at thirteen. Can we talk about it?" (Names in this story have been changed.)

Carol began to cry. Her home was not Christian, and this was the first time she had ever heard about God's standards of morality. I listened as she poured out her heart. She was in a Christian school because her parents wanted a superior academic education for her. Jesus hadn't touched her life yet. As she cried, something in Carol's spirit broke, and she came to Jesus, repentant. Our conversation never left that room. From that time forward, she was a changed girl in class. I realized that the questions she had asked were now answered from a Biblical perspective and would be life-changing for her.

Pleased with the conference with Carol, I then called in Elaine. She was an entirely different story. Belligerent from the onset, she had a "so what" attitude. I reviewed the pledge each student signs upon entering the academy. No student was accepted into the upper grades without a sincere desire to be there. Their pledge included a promise to be morally pure. Any violation in the form of smoking, drinking, or moral impurity demanded immediate expulsion. Elaine readily confessed to violations of the school's code of ethics.

Because of her lack of repentance, I informed Elaine of my decision. "Since it's Friday," I told her, "I'll give you the weekend to pray and think about what you want to do. Until Monday, when we can talk again, I'll not say anything. By then, if there isn't a genuine desire to change, I have no alternative but to inform Mr. Landers of your violation of the academy's pledge." Praying with her and assuring her that I would pray over the weekend that she make Jesus Lord of her life, I dismissed her.

Within an hour, there was no need to pray or wonder about Elaine's decision. It had been made before she ever left my office. The school was soon buzzing with whispered gossip. Looking for sympathy, Elaine had left me and run straight to a male fifth grade teacher with whom her family was acquainted. Instead of directing her to the proper guidance counselor for assistance, he saw the opportunity he had been waiting for.

Fabricating an outrageous story, he phoned Elaine's mother. "You'd better come to the school," he warned. "A teacher said she had a vision and in it saw Elaine involved in immorality. Your daughter is very upset."

Dr. Parker had been extremely antagonistic to me for some time. It all started one morning after I shared a devotion in the teachers' meeting before school. Each teacher was required to take a turn during the year. I had simply shared how I was learning the importance of distinguishing between the written Word of God (*logos* in Greek) and the revealed Word of God *(rhema)*. "Only as the *logos* becomes *rhema* will your life be changed," I said, giving an example from a personal experience.

For some mysterious reason, that little message made Dr. Parker furious. He approached me in the hall later that day and said, "I have my doctorate in theology, and it makes me mad that you could give such a concise talk that was so meaningful!" Unfortunately, his outburst was not a compliment. From that day on, Jim and I seemed to be on the list of people he despised the most. "Jim Stone has no right to pastor," he would say. "He hasn't even been to seminary." We tried to do everything we could to befriend the man but couldn't reach him.

Now he apparently saw his opportunity to remove me permanently from the academy staff. The problem was, his plan backfired. Mr. Landers, informed of the lack of discretion Dr. Parker had used with Elaine, fired him. Elaine, because I now had to reveal the cause of this whole episode, was expelled for breaking the rules.

Furious, Dr. Parker's campaign became a deep, personal vengeance. Angered at being fired from the academy, he went to the Palm Beach Post newspaper. In a few days, splashed across a headline, were the words:

FIRED ACADEMY TEACHER WOULD HELP AGAIN

The text contained statements like, "A fired academy teacher said he would again go through the same procedure that got him fired in order to help a distraught girl.

Dr. John Parker said he was fired because he called the girl's mother onto the campus to help calm the eighth grade girl after a woman teacher had told the student she should be expelled. Parker said the teacher told the girl that the Lord had told her the student had committed immoralities, including smoking and drinking."

The truth was simple. John Parker was fired because of insubordination. If I had truly upset Elaine and all his accusations were true, school procedure had a counselor to deal with the problem. An elementary teacher had no authority to deal with a junior high student. As for Elaine, the Lord didn't have to tell me anything. She had told me all that was necessary for expulsion.

Rumors were rampant. The newspaper called to ask me for a statement. I refused to comment at my husband's and Mr. Landers' request. "God will vindicate you," Jim told me. "Remember, you're still at the school; the guilty ones are not."

That was little comfort at the moment. I really wished I weren't there either. Some students snickered behind their hands when I walked by. Others asked questions I couldn't answer. One night someone used a spray can of red paint and wrote across an academy wall, "FOR A VISION DANDY, SEE SANDEE."

Jim and the children had to be silent, too. It was hard on them to experience my pain and humiliation, but as we prayed together for our enemies, we were strengthened as a family. Personally, I fervently asked, "Lord, will this nightmare never end?"

Finally, with the passing of time, the gossipers seemed to be satisfied, and life at the academy returned to some degree of normalcy.

Now, weeks later, these horrible notes. How could I help but wonder if there was a connection between John Parker's firing, Elaine's expulsion, and these events. Was it their dismissals referred to in the note?

What about the L.E.W? Was it a hoax or the invention of a sick mind? I read on in the series of notes the FBI agent had handed me. One was an explanation of the alleged organization:

1.    L.E.W. is an underground terrorist organization.

2.    There is at least one connection in each of the United States.

3.    There are six major headquarters.....

4.    There are many small branches of L.E.W. that employ children and young adults who specialize in revenge, perhaps for a fellow member or friend. They are given a job which they must complete by a certain deadline. The job could be a number of things. For instance: knifing someone, continuous harassment, setting fire to or breaking into a house, or just plain writing notes."

The note went on describing the activities of the group. Threats were made against our family.

"Lord Jesus, you are our defender. When the enemy surrounds us like a flood, we will trust in you. Please reveal the guilty party," we prayed.

Mr. Landers held a high school assembly after the bomb threat. The essence of his message was simple.

*"He that covereth his sins shall not prosper, but whosoever confesseth and forsaketh them shall have mercy"* (Proverbs 28:13).

The unified prayers of so many concerned people were quickly answered. The next time I arrived at school, the office area was a hubbub of crying girls and ashen-faced parents. One mother whom I knew cried out, "Oh, SanDee, I'm so sorry for what Gayle has done!"

Grieving, I thought, *Oh no! Not Gayle! She's one of my sweetest students.*

As the story unfolded, the truth was revealed. Two of my students, both eighth graders, were responsible for the notes. Valerie wrote them, and Gayle made the delivery. A third girl knew about their plot and felt the pressure of conviction. "If you don't confess, I will," she told Gayle and Valerie. They finally relented and went to Mr. Landers.

Valerie, a brilliant girl, was undergoing psychiatric care. A disturbed child, she had voraciously read about Patricia Hearst and the Symbionese Liberation Army's activities. She had patterned the LEW notes after media reports in newspapers and on television.

Gayle, siding with Valerie in the belief that Elaine and John Parker had been unjustly dismissed, decided to retaliate in their defense. She was easy prey to Valerie's persuasive schemes.

Two more were added to the dismissal list. Gayle and Valerie must reap what they had sown.

I was counting the days until the end of the school year. I hadn't planned to teach again next year, and now I never wanted to teach again. God had given me some wonderful insights into His plan for women, but I was sure that these truths would be forever hidden in my heart. Little did I realize that I'd soon be teaching a successful women's Bible study.

Jesus reminded me of a prayer I had recently prayed. I had asked Him to teach me to obey His Word. "How can you bless your enemies, or do good to those who despitefully use you, or be thankful in ALL things if you never have an enemy or have someone who wrongs you or have a time to be thankful when problems come your way?" He asked.

My heart response was a commitment to pray for Elaine, Valerie, Gayle, and Dr. Parker whenever they came to mind. God had been our defender - a very present help in time of trouble. I could truly thank Him for that. For three years, I remembered to pray for Dr. Parker. We had no idea what had ever become of him.

### December 1977

Loryn had come home from Bethany for the holidays. "Mom, do you think that Dr. Parker has ever repented for what he did to you?" she asked, out of the blue.

Surprised that she even thought about him anymore, I considered her question. Finally, I replied, "No, I don't think so. If he had ever repented, I'd have heard from him."

The next afternoon, the phone rang and I answered it. A man said, "Mrs. Stone, when I tell you who this is, please don't hang up."

My immediate response was, "I won't, Dr. Parker."

John Parker went on to relate a story that forever impressed me with God's love for one wayward individual. "I called to ask your forgiveness," he said. "I know now that I wasn't even saved when I worked at the academy. I had a lot of head knowledge but no relationship with Jesus. Last week I was riding in my car when, all of a sudden, the Holy Spirit came in and convicted me of my evil heart. I began to cry so hard that I pulled over to the side of the road to repent. Please let me make things right with you and Jim."

Saul had his encounter with Jesus on the road to Damascus. John Parker had his on a road in Oklahoma! They were both changed men and that was what really mattered.

Jim, who had been considered worthless before, and treated as such, was now "Reverend" Stone, or "sir," in phone conversations with John. We were thrilled at the convicting and cleansing power of the Holy Spirit.

It wasn't as easy for John Parker to forgive himself. He called often, even offering Jim positions in a Christian school he had founded.

The guilt he was holding onto was apparent, and we prayed that he'd receive the forgiveness that God, and we, offered freely. It finally happened after we moved to New York. Calling us, John asked if he could visit. When he did, he stood in front of our church the Sunday morning that he was there and publicly repented in front of our congregation. We didn't need that. We had forgiven him a long time ago, but he needed to free his spirit. After that visit, we never heard from him again.

### Clappers and Tigers

When hunters go on safari, a necessary element of the hunt is a band of natives called clappers. The function of these clappers is to run through the bush in an agitating manner to flush out the hidden tigers. Once seen, the hunter can shoot them. In life, there are many tigers that hide in the recesses of our heart - anger, resentment, jealousy, bitterness, etc. God sends clappers to flush out the tigers. A "clapper" may be a family member or friend. It may be a slow driver in traffic or an ornery boss at work. Many times, our tendency is to shoot the clapper instead of the tiger.

Defending myself, instead of allowing God to be my defense, is something I have had to deal with over and over again. As I review many of the clappers in my life, I trust I have learned to shoot the tiger.

Many people have served this position of clapper well. It's sometimes difficult to be a fish swimming upstream and not defend your actions. It would be so much easier to turn around and "go with the flow," but I can't.

*"Enter in at the narrow gate; for wide is the gate, and broad is the way, that leadeth to destruction, and many there be who go in that way; Because narrow is the gate, and hard is the way, which leadeth into life, and few there be that find it"* (Matthew 7:13,14).

Not defending the reasons that I don't listen to certain jokes, read secular books, watch TV, or go certain places has many times caused me to be labeled a "prude." Not wanting to appear self-righteous or to compromise my convictions, the tigers of anger and hurt sometimes surface. As a Christian, I realize that my convictions can't be explained or defended. They are deeply personal, and God wants me to walk them out in a quiet and peaceable way.

*"Ye are the light of the world.... Let your light so shine before men, that they may see your good works, and glorify your Father, who is in heaven"* (Matthew 5:14a,16).

A light doesn't talk; it shines to illuminate the dark places. *May my life always shine for you, Lord Jesus, and draw those wanting to know you.*

Dr. Jackson served as a clapper during my child-bearing years. I knew I was going to have four children. Retaliating in anger or frustration, because he looked at my condition from a purely medical point of view, would have been fruitless. Allowing the tigers of unbelief and doubt to consume my heart would have negated God's promise. I shot those tigers, not Dr. Jackson. In time, God vindicated me with the birth of four children.

The church elders served as clappers in Jim's life. Had he "shot" them, he never would have sought God for my healing. The tigers of confusion, hurt, and indignation would have lived instead. The clappers meant no harm, but the tigers, allowed to live, could have destroyed him.

*"A good man out of the good treasure of the heart bringeth forth good things, and an evil man out of the evil treasure bringeth forth evil things"* (Matthew 12:35).

When Jim left RCA, the clappers seemed to come out of the bush in droves and scared up many tigers. How could Jim defend the position he was taking? Leaving a secure job when you have four children and a wife, to see if a Bible verse really works, is foolhardy. His only defense was, "I think we can seek first the kingdom of God and trust Him to provide for our needs. Watch our lives. If it doesn't work, I'll be the first to admit it." What else could he say?

Jim and I have made many decisions for governing our lives that have been mocked, ridiculed, and derided. Others had the freedom to do things we could not, and God alone would have to defend us. We are walking out the walk to which God has called us. All persons,

Christians or non-believers, will stand before Him someday and answer for responses to His calling in their lives.

A sister-in-law approached Loryn at thirteen years old. "Your parents are so strict with you. If you ever have a problem and need to talk, come to me." That offer could have scared the tiger of rebellion out of our daughter's heart. The tiger wasn't there, however, and the clapper turned away, unfulfilled.

When Loryn, Tim, Jeff and Bonnie were in school, we faced criticism for having them in a Christian school. When Joshua came along and we decided to home-school, the clappers were on every corner. "What about socialization?" we were asked. "Doesn't he need friends?"

We tried simply to answer, not defend, "Yes, friends of our choosing. Peer groups have a pretty poor track record, you know."

Others confronted us with our lack of education. "Do you have a degree in education? What about high school; how can you teach chemistry or trigonometry?"

Our only defense could be, "We think we're doing what God asked us to do. We'll check with Him about our qualifications and the future. Watch and see if it works."

The internal tigers that would shake our confidence were, one by one, shot and buried.

Church in our home in Florida, and in our red barn in New York, gave the clappers a field day. We were so unconventional. Defending the reasons we did some things differently would have been an exercise in futility.

We didn't have a Sunday School in our churches. Never critical of those who did, we were maligned because we didn't. I personally felt the sting of criticism in the early days of church in our home. It was a new concept to me, too.

At one time, the Lord used my husband as a clapper in my life. Loryn was baby-sitting for a neighborhood family and came home with a request. "Mr. Williams asked if he can send his little girl, Sally, to our Sunday School. I didn't tell him we didn't have one. I just said I'd ask you, Dad."

Jim's answer was to the point, "No, he can't send Sally. I'll go down and talk to Larry." Grabbing his Bible and a children's Bible story book, Jim turned to me and said, "Come with me." The tigers of embarrassment, irritation, and rebellion quickly rose up in my heart. "How can you say 'no'?" I inquired. "You know that the Williamses don't go to church. Don't you care if we reach their child with the gospel?" I didn't want to go to their house with Jim!

"Trust me," was Jim's short reply.

I decided to shoot the tigers and obey my husband. In my heart, I knew I **could** trust him, but I wondered how he was going to handle this situation without offending Larry and Jan. We walked down the lane to the Williamses' home. Larry cordially invited us in, and his wife, Janice, offered us a glass of iced tea. Once the preliminary amenities were taken care of, the four of us sat down in the living room. Jim jumped right into the subject at hand. Turning to Larry, he said, "Loryn mentioned that you want to send Sally to our Sunday School. First of all, I want you to know that we don't have a Sunday School. We gather together as families, keeping the children with us. Secondly, I wouldn't want to rob you of the wonderful responsibility God has given to you as a father to teach Sally about Him."

"But I don't know anything about the Bible," Larry honestly admitted.

"I thought about that possibility," was Jim's reply. Holding out the Bible story book, he continued. "Perhaps you can read this book to Sally. It will give her a basis for knowing what the Bible is all about, and you and Jan will gain some understanding, too."

Jim didn't invite them to church. He didn't preach to them about their need for Jesus. He just gave them a kid's book. They eagerly received it, agreeing to read to Sally, and we left.

We were thrilled to glance out the sliding glass door of the family room one Sunday morning a few weeks later to see the whole Williams family walking toward our house. They never missed a church service after that. Before long, Larry, Jan, and Sally all had committed their lives to Christ. There was no need for Jim to defend his actions. He obeyed his conviction, and God honored it.

Jim was ridiculed for walking to work for seven weeks when our car was wrecked. The Lord had led him to wait for His provision instead of going into debt for another car. The man in New York who mocked him became another clapper in my life. Pride was the biggest tiger that welled up in my heart. I didn't want my husband to look like a fool! I came really close that time to shooting the clapper. I couldn't defend Jim; I was too humiliated. When I simply decided to stand with him, the tiger ran away.

### Joshua's *Bar Mitzvah*  February 1992

Long before Joshua's thirteenth birthday, Jim and I began to discuss the possibility of having a *Bar Mitzvah* for him. In recent years I had been blessed to see Christians explore their Jewish roots. In many churches, Passover *seders* were being held to educate believers in the deeper meaning of this feast. Many Christian song writers began writing minor-key Jewish music. The words focused on the Psalms and Old Testament truths. I had often wondered why the church had become so Gentile when it started out so Jewish. I missed the spiritually significant elements of my heritage. *Bar Mitzvah* was one of those occasions.

As we considered the true meaning of this celebration, we felt sure that it could be a blessing in Josh's life. *Bar Mitzvah* literally means "Son of the Commandment," representing the time when a young man comes into personal accountability to God. He is allowed to participate in reading the *torah* (scriptures) in the synagogue service, and he is now responsible to God for his own actions.

Planning this celebration became a deeply personal event for me. Joshua was asked to choose a passage of scripture to govern his future life. He was to write a speech to deliver to gathered friends and family explaining what this day means to him. Our son Jeff wrote a song for Jim to sing to Josh.

A few weeks before this special day, I was in Florida for the birth of a grandson. My brother came to see the new baby on the same night that Jeff gave me a tape of the song he had written for Joshua. Sure that my brother would be thrilled, I shared our plans and the taped song with him. He wasn't thrilled. He was furious and railed out at me.

"You can't do that. You aren't Jewish." He went on and on informing me why I couldn't do this, and I went on and on telling him why I could! Hurt, I shot the clapper this time. My brother hadn't been involved in Judaism for years. He now professed to be an atheist. How dare he! The tigers of fury, indignation, and rage flew out of my heart unchecked. It was not a nice scene, but before it was over, I recouped and shot the tigers in repentance. I apologized to my brother for my outburst.

Joshua's *Bar Mitzvah* wasn't typical. So many Jewish celebrations I had attended concentrated on a big party with lots of gifts. The spiritual significance had been lost. We held Joshua's *Bar Mitzvah* in the church fellowship hall with special people in his life invited to rejoice with us. The most important guest was Jesus, and we think He was pleased. Jim sang the song Jeff had written:

When a Boy Becomes a Man
I have cared for you and carried you,
All across the land.
I've played with you, prayed with you,
As you've held my hand.
I've watched you grow, as you know,
Together we have walked.
Son of mine, there comes a time,
We must have a talk.

You're thirteen now, I can allow
My hand to slip away.
It's time for more to reach out for
Our Father's hand today.
Now it's time to start the climb,
Holding to His hand.
In God's grace, you're at the place
When a boy becomes a man.

There's a time - you've been getting near it,
There's a time to listen to the Spirit.
He will guide you; with wisdom you will hear it,
That's the time when a boy becomes a man.
I'll let go of your heart and hand now,
It's the way our Father made His plan now,
Before His throne, alone you will stand now;
That's the time a boy becomes a man.

I will stay by you, pray for you,
Stand right by your side.
I'll still talk with you, walk with you,
But our Lord will be your guide.
I'll be near, don't ever fear,
If you should need a hand.
But realize that in my eyes,
Before God now, you're a man.

After Jim's song, I read the poem that I was given about a mother's love for an adopted child (Chapter 2). It was difficult to read with all the emotions it stirred, but I stumbled tearfully through it.

Then, Joshua, nervous but poised, delivered the speech he had written:

*"Trust in the Lord with all thine heart; and lean not unto thine own understanding. In all thy ways acknowledge him, and he shall direct thy paths'"* (Proverbs 3:5,6).

"As I look towards manhood, I have chosen this verse to be 'a lamp unto my feet and a light unto my path.' This time of my life is exciting and also a little fearful. The exciting part is that I am going into manhood and I will be able to do some things I haven't been able to do as a child. The fearful part is that I must answer to God for the things I do. In answering to God, I want Him to find me guiltless of any sin."

"This is a time for me to start seriously thinking about the Word of God. I must look in the Bible for some of my answers in life, But when I have a problem I can't get through, I still will go to my Dad for advice. Sometimes it helps to talk to someone who may have faced the same problem. The words *Bar Mitzvah* mean 'Son of the Commandment.' It is the time when Jewish boys are allowed to read from the holy scriptures. This event is marking the time when I am to put what I read in the Bible to practice."

"Part of growing older is a change in the way I act. I **Corinthians 13:11** says, *'When I was a child, I talked like a child; When I became a man, I put childish ways behind me.'* I will become more self-conscious of the way I act around younger children. I realize I am their example and leader, and I want the parents to appreciate my being with them. It is also important that I remember my friends and think unselfishly about them. I know myself that it's nice to be thought about by others. I ask you to remind me when I slack off."

"I would like to thank my family for taking me as their child. My name, Joshua, means "God saves," and I know He has indeed saved me."

The speech went on to thank others present for their influence in Josh's life.

None of my Jewish relatives attended, but that was okay. My heart was so full of praise to God that this day needed no defense. Joshua was touched in a special way, and his life will glorify his Lord.

**Sulfur Springs, Arkansas  June 6, 1993**

### THE FAMILY JOURNAL

**Familiar Group of Stones**
**Sighted in Northwest Arkansas**
By M.R. Related/correspondent

Startled northwest Arkansas citizens give eyewitness accounts of seeing many odd-shaped stones, arranged in mysterious order. WHAT COULD IT MEAN?

A service station attendant was quoted on Friday as saying, "I can't hardly believe it!... It's as if there was some kinda divine plan to get 'em all to the same place at the same time."

The group consisted of a colorful assortment of sizes, shapes, and varieties. From the southern quadrant, there came Thad and Loryn (Stone) Smith along with some smaller smiths, Christopher, Isaak, Micah, Amy, and Jacob. From the same peninsula came Jeff and Laila Stone with their pebbles, Jessica, Levi, and Aslan.

The northeastern specimens consisted of Chris and Bonnie (Stone) Chiarot and their three female chiarots, Katy, Melissa, and Laura.

The midwest variety contributed Rich and Marnie Stone. Among the local variety were Tim and Karen Stone with their small stones, Nathanael and Anna. A medium sized stone, Joshua, stood close to what appeared to be the most ancient of the group, Jim and SanDee Stone. WHAT COULD THIS MEAN? Experts agree that it must have the makings of a STONE FAMILY REUNION.

All of that was printed on the front of a stack of t-shirts...

It began when I said, "Tim, could you design a simple logo for t-shirts for our family reunion?" I had in mind a few balloons, the date, and STONE FAMILY REUNION on the front of each shirt.

"That won't do at all, Mom. It's got to be something the guys will wear. Let me think about it." was Tim's reply.

Handing Tim the t-shirts, white for the kids and red for the adults, I relented. When you ask a creative artist to do something simple, it just isn't within the realm of possibility. The shirts were returned to me with a picture of Stonehenge gracing the front and followed by the foregoing "simple logo." Truthfully, everyone was much happier with Tim's design than they would have been with my balloons!

The whole family was present, and as we sat around the large living room of Harbor House (A Christian guest-house) that first evening after everyone had arrived, Jim and I felt blessed beyond measure. We were a family united in Christ. This was all we could have ever hoped for.

I remembered the lady many years ago who warned me, "You're going to have four rebellious teenagers at one time!" My answer to her was, "No I won't. These children are all an answer to prayer, and dedicated to God. They are His, and they will be trained to love and serve Him."

*"Train up a child in the way he should go and, when he is old, he will not depart from it"* (Proverbs 22:6).

Each child had his own personal encounter with Christ at an early age, and each had a time when that commitment was tested. The outward circumstances were always an opportunity for Jim and me to remind them that they were an answer to prayer and were marked for the Master's use even before they were born.

The week at Harbor House was one we will long cherish in our memories. We played games, swam in the pond in the park next door, and the little children waded in the creek. We ate heartily, sang together, and each morning, one of the men was responsible for a daily devotional. There were serious conversations and a lot of laughter, too.

With fourteen children (counting Uncle Josh) in the house, there was also a great deal of happy noise!

All the people we told "watch us and see," would be constrained to agree with us.    We sought first the kingdom of God and His righteousness and trusted Him to provide.    Our family today is His defense that He is true to His Word.

## Chapter Nine

## Acknowledging Him as Protector

*"God is our refuge and strength, a very present help in trouble"* (Psalm 46:1).

### West Palm Beach, Florida 1959

"De Lawd protected y'all. It was a miracle!" the wide-eyed observer exclaimed as we all struggled out of the water.

Our Sunday School class of young adults was on a hayride on the back of an open flatbed truck. We were slowly traveling down a shell-rock road along a canal. Singing, talking, and laughing, we were oblivious to any possible danger. Without warning, the bank gave way, dumping the group of us into the water. The elderly man fishing on the canal bank had observed the truck teetering on the edge until we were all thrown free from danger. The truck then fell with a splash into the canal.

Extremely excited, the witness to the accident rambled on in amazement. "De truck just hung dere on its side 'til everybody was moved out of de way. Den de Lawd turned it loose and let 'er fall. It was a MIRACLE!" he repeated.

My personal danger was my heroic husband's attempt to rescue me. The hay had fallen on top of us. I was struggling to get free when my brave rescuer pushed me deeper under the water, trying to get me into a 'lifesaving' position! In a few minutes, he realized that the water was only shoulder deep, and he let me go so that I could scramble up the bank!

The hayride that started as a time of carefree fun ended up a sober time of praise to our God for His protection. Our new baby, Loryn, could have been orphaned that evening.

### Jackson Hole, Wyoming August 2, 1976

"Dad, can we climb?" That question from Tim and Jeff resounded in our ears almost every day for five weeks. Once we left the flat lands of Florida, every little hill or rock became a potential opportunity for the boys to climb.  We were on a bicentennial trip to the western part of our country, and the chances to climb were endless.  If we had stopped as often as they begged, we would have never seen the Grand Canyon in Arizona, the great Sequoia trees in California, or Mt. Rainier in Washington state!

Many times, though, Jim did stop and allow the "boys to be boys."  Arriving in Jackson Hole, Wyoming, on a sunny summer day, the familiar refrain resumed.  "Look at the neat hills!  Can we climb.  Please, Dad.  Please!" Tim implored.

Jim, much more understanding than I of the insatiable desire in the boys to climb and explore, had an idea, "I'll leave Mom and the girls in town to shop and take you to the outskirts of town to climb."  As Loryn, Bonnie and I got out of the car, Jim said, "Meet me on this corner at noon.  If we aren't there then, give us another hour.  We'll be back by one o'clock for sure."

"Don't let them do anything dangerous," I admonished as they drove away.

I imagined I could hear the boys groan, "Aw Mom.  We're **always** careful!"

*Mothers are definitely more protective than Dads,* I thought.  I had played my one string banjo of 'be careful' practically every time the boys got out of the car.  I was sure they were tired of hearing it.  I needed to relax and change my tune!

The girls and I meandered down the main street, wandering through interesting shops and trying not to stare at the many "real" cowboys we saw.  We were perplexed at strange stuffed animals, called jackalopes, that we saw in many shop windows.  They looked like jack rabbits, but had horns like antelope.  It was a while before even I realized that they were a fabricated local joke.  Laughing at our gullibility, we realized it was soon time to meet Jim and the boys.

We stood looking in the direction they had driven two hours before.  Our car wasn't in sight.  "The guys probably needed the extra hour to get today's climbing out of their systems," I told the girls.  "Let's just window shop in the vicinity so that we can watch for them."

One o'clock arrived, and we were hungry and tired.    Lunch would be a welcome respite for my aching feet.    "I'll bet Tim and Jeff are starved if they've been climbing all this time," I commented.    Back to the corner we trooped, but our car wasn't to be seen.    Fear began to grip my heart.    *Where were they?*

Then, much to my relief, I saw the car coming down the street. As it drew nearer, I noticed that there was only one person in the front seat.    *Maybe the boys are lying down in the back.*    I hopefully thought. As Jim screeched to a halt opposite us, his white and perspiring face revealed the truth.    The boys weren't with him.

"Where are Tim and Jeff?" I fearfully asked.

"Get in quickly," was Jim's reply.    As we drove away, he told me what had happened.    "We found a good climbing hill, and I instructed the boys to go to the top, turn around, and come back down. I sat in the car to wait for them.    By noon, they were nowhere in sight, and I started to climb a small rise to look for them.    It was a whole lot steeper than I thought.    The height of these hills is really deceiving. When I got to the top of the rise, I realized that the hill I told them to climb went up, and up, and up.    I couldn't see that from the vantage point at the bottom."

We drove back to the area where Jim had released the boys.    It would have been good if I had known then about the passage of scripture concerning casting down imaginings, but I didn't.    Inside, I was in a turmoil.    I imagined cliffs for the boys to fall over and all kinds of wild animals to attack them.    Furious at Jim for exposing our sons to danger, I silently tried to deal with my feelings.

*Jim loves them as much as you do.    He wouldn't purposely try to hurt them.    He's suffering, too.    Help him.    If you don't forgive him, you may never see the boys again.*    These sobering thoughts had to be the Lord speaking to me, and they captured my attention.    The anger instantly subsided and, silently, I forgave him.    Then I could objectively join in prayer.

The four of us prayed that Tim and Jeff would be protected.    Jim remembered seeing a sheriff's helicopter flying overhead when we were in town.    "We'll wait until two o'clock.    If we don't see the boys by then, I'll check on the possibility of getting the helicopter to search for them," Jim said.

We sat in the car, enough of a distance away that we could see the whole hill. Our eyes were glued to the area in which they had climbed.

At exactly two o'clock, we reluctantly decided to head out for the sheriff's office in town. I took one last, hopeful look at the hill as Jim's hand began turning the ignition key. I noticed two tiny dots way up at the top! They were moving! "There they are!" I shouted. How we praised God! We sat watching as the dots drew closer and closer and turned into the images of our sons. In a short time, crying with relief, we embraced the boys. We couldn't be upset at them. They had climbed to the top and turned around, just as they had been told.

Jeff, with a completely grumpy countenance, murmured. "I'll never go climbing with Tim again." We were so relieved to have them safely back, that we didn't even question why.

Years later, the whole story of the adventure came out. The boys had found a sleeping bag with a body in it. Just as they were going to kick it, a sleepy camper emerged. The boys thought it was a dead body! Later, they found a dead animal's remains, and Tim wanted to track the living animal that had killed it. Jeff, our cautious one, went along with the adventure until Tim wanted to see if he could jump across a deep ravine. At this point, Jeff's level head probably saved his brother's life. I trembled when I thought of what could have happened if I hadn't been willing to forgive.

*"And be ye kind one to another, tenderhearted, forgiving one another, even as God, for Christ's sake, hath forgiven you"* (Ephesians 4:32).

### Columbus, Ohio  March 1989

Jim was traveling on the interstate highway in a twenty-four foot Ryder truck when we moved to Arkansas from New York. He was in front of me in the morning rush-hour traffic. As I followed him in our mini-van, I struggled to stay in the same lane so that we wouldn't become separated.

Suddenly, a tailgate flew off a pickup truck in front of Jim. The traffic was bumper to bumper in all three lanes headed west. He was in the center lane and couldn't swerve left or right to avoid the tailgate. The Ryder truck hit it, slinging it back toward the van. Jim wasn't even aware of the danger I was in. I immediately heard a loud thumping noise and, somehow, was able to get to the shoulder to investigate. Both tires on the passenger side had been slashed and were flat. I never felt the van falter, and how I managed to cross the lane of heavy traffic was a mystery!

*"For he shall give his angels charge over thee, to keep thee in all thy ways"*        (Psalm 91:11).

Jim, glancing in the rear view mirror, realized that I was no longer behind him. He pulled over to the shoulder and left the truck. He walked back to where I stood in bewilderment.

A policeman soon stopped to assist us, and the truck driver who had caused the accident returned for his tailgate. Before long, we were on our way with new tires provided by the company that owned the truck. We were delayed for an hour but none the worse for the wear. *Thank you, Lord, for watching over us.*

Leaving the motel the next morning, I noticed our Christian music cassette tapes strewn all over the front of the van floor. It was obvious that someone had broken into the van. My heart sank as I remembered the things stored in the back of the van - our good china and crystal, silverware, and my jewelry box. On closer inspection, the only thing we could find missing was a handful of change from the ashtray! "Wow!" I exclaimed. "I wish I could have seen the size of those angels protecting our van!"

### Huntsville, Arkansas  1989

There were two things I had hoped to do when we moved to Arkansas. The first was to learn to quilt. The second was to apprentice as a midwife.

A quilting class, and resulting project of a sampler quilt for our guest room, completed the first wish.

Soon after moving, I was introduced to a Christian midwife who agreed to apprentice me. Thrilled, I became available for many adventures in these Arkansas hills.

One of the first deliveries where I assisted was in a cabin with no electricity or running water. It was miles out on an unpaved mountain road. It was in such an obscure area that we made a trial run to be sure we'd be able to find our destination when the time came.

The call came at 9:30 on a December night. Turning off the pavement an hour later, we were confident we could find the cabin. After all, we had easily found it in daylight. Soon, the road narrowed to little more than a rocky path, and I was beginning to get nervous.

"Nancy, are you sure we're on the right road?" I asked.

"No," she replied, "but I've still got a map in the trunk." Stopping, she took a flashlight out of the glove compartment and went around to the back of the car. Just as she popped open the trunk lid, a bloodcurdling scream pierced the darkness. Grabbing the map, she jumped back into the driver's seat and firmly locked the door. "What was **that**?" she asked.

"I think it was a panther!" was my terrified reply. "They sound like a woman screaming."

"I thought maybe we were close to Tara and Bob's house, and she screamed!" Nancy responded.

Both of us were thoroughly frightened as she turned the car around and we backtracked to the road we had missed. Way out in front of us, we saw a dim light from the solar-powered light in Tara's cabin. In the pitch-black darkness, nothing ever looked quite so good!

That night, a healthy baby girl was born, in spite of the lack of modern conveniences. We never took the safe birth of a baby for granted. We were so aware of the need for God's protection. It was a long way to a hospital from these mountain hideaways.

All I could think was, *If only my mother could see me now. She always thought I was a little crazy. Now she'd be convinced!*

**St. Petersburg, Florida  February 1992**

I became interested in midwifery when I attended the birth of two of Loryn's children. Micah was born in a birthing center, and Amy was born at home. Both babies were delivered by midwives, and I was very impressed by the personal, non-intervening care. I wanted to have the skills necessary to assist Christians whenever circumstances warranted my services.

By the time Loryn's fifth child was due, I had been apprenticing as a midwife for some time and had delivered three babies on my own. "Mom, what would you think about flying to Florida to deliver our baby?" Loryn cheerfully asked.

I didn't have an immediate reply. *Could I be objective enough to deliver my own grandchild?* I wondered. *It would be an honor, but maybe I'd be too nervous.*

"You ask Thad to pray about it, and I'll ask Daddy," I replied. "Our husbands' answers will be God's answer for us. If they agree, I'll have the faith to do it, knowing that we'd be covered by God's protection." Assuring her of my gratitude for asking me, we agreed to wait for our husbands to hear from God. Soon, both men felt it would be a good experience for Loryn and me.

I flew to Florida a week before the baby was due. Loryn, in the meantime, had good prenatal care from a physician throughout her pregnancy, and everything was in order. Her due date was February 3.

On the fifth, we began to get anxious. I had asked Jim to pray specifically that Loryn deliver on that date. The morning came, and there were no imminent signs of labor. Jim phoned early in the morning to see what was happening. Loryn informed him, "**Nothing** is happening. You were supposed to pray that I'd have the baby today!"

"The day isn't over," he replied. "I'm still praying for a fast, safe delivery - today!" Nobody is more unsettled than a pregnant woman who is past her due date; my daughter, no exception. Every second is magnified with discomfort and anxiety.

"Let's get someone to watch the children, and we'll go shopping and out to lunch," I suggested.

We arrived home from our excursion in time to start dinner and prepare for the Wednesday night church service. Loryn was tired but in better spirits. Thad arrived at six, and we hurriedly ate.

While clearing the table, Loryn excused herself to use the bathroom. I continued to do the dishes for some time, then realized that she had not come out yet. Quickly drying my hands, I knocked on the bathroom door. "Are you all right?" I asked.

"No!" was the breathless reply from the other side of the door! It didn't take much intuition to recognize her hard breathing through a contraction. Her water had broken, and the intensity of labor began without warning.

We had had a very calm plan for the delivery of this baby. Thad's Mom would come to get the other children and take them to her house, if they were awake. Two of Loryn's church friends would come to assist me.

Now there was no time to formulate plan B! "Thad!" I yelled. "Get the kids to the back bedroom, get a mattress on the floor outside the bathroom door, and get water boiling for the instruments!"

Thad responded like a pro to my militant orders! He helped to assist Loryn the few feet from the bathroom to the mattress. Then he instructed Christopher to watch the little ones and dropped my bulb syringe, scissors, and bellybutton clamp into the boiling water. There was no time to call anyone!

Loryn was settled on the mattress in a matter of minutes. "Mom, I'll never be able to do it," she said, looking up pleadingly at me. "It's so intense." The contractions piled one on top of the other, with little time in between.

As soon as the current contraction began to subside, I prepared to examine her. "There's no need to worry, honey," I said, feeling the baby's head in the birth canal. "It won't be long. The baby is almost here."

Seconds later, eight pound Jacob Matthew made his unceremonious entry into the world.

Jacob (Jack) was named for my dad who had died the previous year. Loryn had promised my mom that, if the baby was a boy, she would name him after my dad. In Judaism, you never name a baby after someone living, but after the dead, to carry on their name. My delivering Jacob and his being named after my dad was a great blessing to my mother.

When we called Jim to tell him the good news, I jokingly said, "Next time, we'll ask you to pray for a safe delivery. Forget the fast!"

There had been no time to get nervous. The Lord had protected even my emotions. Loryn and I had shared the most intimate experience possible between a mother and daughter. *Lord, you are so good to me.*

### Huntsville, Arkansas  February 27, 1993

As we tumbled into bed at 1:00 A.M., my last drowsy words to Jim were, "I hope Peggy doesn't go into labor tonight. I'm so tired!"

That day, some friends from Pennsylvania with their seven children had arrived for a visit. The evening had been spent catching up on all the news. We visited longer than we should have, and now I needed a good night's sleep in anticipation of Peggy's soon-to-arrive baby.

At four in the morning, we were awakened by the jangling phone. "Peggy's in labor. Come quickly!"

Trying to shake myself out of the stupor of deep sleep, I threw on some clothes and called my friend Mary, who was to assist me. I gathered my bag of supplies and headed out the door. The cold night air shocked me into wakefulness. I was grateful for that!

It took half an hour to drive to Peggy's house. All the way there, I fervently prayed for her and the baby. I had two prayer requests. *Please let the baby breathe spontaneously,* and *don't let Peggy hemorrhage.*

My mind flew back to a nightmare I had experienced two months before. In it, I saw Peggy being wheeled into a hospital room. She was enclosed in an oxygen tent with a doctor standing nearby. He informed me, "We almost lost Peggy. She hemorrhaged when you delivered her." Viewing Peggy through the plastic of the tent, I saw that she was colorless and not moving.

"Jim!" I cried, as I shook him awake. "I can't deliver Peggy's baby." I was shaking from the realism of the nightmare. I went on to tell my husband about it.

Once he was awake enough to focus on what I was saying, Jim told me that I had the dream, not so that I wouldn't deliver the baby, but so that we would know how to pray. "If the Lord doesn't want you to deliver the baby, He can intervene. In the meantime, you know that fear is not of God," Jim instructed.

Every day from that time on, we prayed that Peggy wouldn't hemorrhage.

I tried to rest in Jim's reassurance but many times in those two months, I must admit, I secretly prayed another prayer. *Lord, please intervene if I'm not to deliver this baby.*

There were many opportunities for the Lord to intervene. Peggy's due date was March 1. On February 15, we had a sixteen-inch snowfall. I couldn't have gotten down off our mountain if I had wanted to! Then the snow melted a week later when it rained, and the weather turned warm. On February 20, I had a speaking engagement in southern Arkansas. The Lord had another chance to prevent me from delivering the baby.

Now, as I drove to town, I rested in the assurance that this was His will. I was supposed to deliver the baby, and I knew only God would be my protection. The hospital in Huntsville was permanently closed, and the nearest hospital was almost thirty miles away. I had forgotten that Frank and Peggy didn't even have a telephone.

Mary had already gotten there by the time I arrived and had the crock pot on for hot compresses and water boiling in a pan for the instruments. Peggy was well on her way to full dilation when I examined her.

There is always such an exhilaration in preparing for a birth, but even more so with this one. I already had been a part of both a spiritual and physical birth in this family. Peggy, her husband, Frank, and two older boys, Jesse and Ben, had been birthed into the Kingdom of God in our church in New York. After they moved to Arkansas, I had delivered their son Noah, now 20 months old. In a very short time, another child would join their family!

A few weeks before, Peggy and I had gone to the health unit for her last prenatal examination. The nurse practitioner who thoroughly examined her informed us that everything was fine. She listened to the baby's strong heartbeat with a Doppler stethoscope. "This baby is a big one," she reported. That was no surprise to us, as Noah had weighed a hefty nine pounds.

Now, as I felt this baby's head in the birth canal, I thought to myself, *this feels like a very small head.* It was a fleeting thought, but in a few minutes, with one last push, a crying, black-haired, tiny baby girl, Grace, emerged. After three boys, we rejoiced that it was a girl. I was very surprised that the baby **was** so small. *She surely doesn't come close to nine pounds,* I thought.

Peggy expressed amazement that Grace's birth had been so easy but, in a few minutes, she was in agony with harder contractions than she had with the delivery. "Please get the baby off me," she begged. "I'm hurting so bad." The baby was lying across her belly as I waited for the umbilical cord to stop pulsing. The cord became still, so I quickly cut it and handed Grace to Mary to wrap in a receiving blanket and cap. I needed to devote my full attention to Peggy.

"It's probably the placenta. Give a little push," I encouraged. All of a sudden, a whitish-blue blob began to emerge. *What is this?* I wondered. Then I remembered a birth I had attended with Nancy. The baby had been born in the unbroken amniotic sac. That picture superimposed itself over this present image. "It's another baby!" I shouted, seeing black hair through the sac. Glancing up at Peggy, I saw her turn pale. Afraid she would faint at the shock, I encouraged, "It's okay, Peggy. Take a deep breath; you're doing great!" I hastily tore the sac open, and with another little push, Sarah was born, head down and squalling. She was a carbon copy of her sister. A sterilized shoe lace from little brother Noah's shoe to tie her cord and a sock from big brother Jesse to keep her head warm did just fine!

For the next hour, all I could think of was the nightmare I had two months before. That memory made me work very hard to keep

Peggy's uterus firm to avoid excessive bleeding. Peggy didn't know about the dream and kept begging me to quit massaging her uterus. I couldn't and inwardly cried because I knew I was hurting her. "It's good that the contractions are so hard, Peg. Hang in there. It'll be over soon," I implored. It took an hour before the placenta was delivered, but there was no hemorrhaging.

Grace weighed in at 6 pounds and 4 ounces. Sarah weighed 6 pounds and 7 ounces. They were perfect healthy little girls.

Had twins been suspected, I couldn't have delivered them. It's against the law for a midwife to knowingly deliver multiple births in Arkansas. Although I chose not to seek state licensing, in good conscience I would have refused because of the possible dangers in multiple births. The Lord prevented an experienced professional, with a much more sophisticated stethoscope than I have, from hearing two heartbeats. He not only protected Peggy, the babies and me, but prevented a huge medical bill that they couldn't have paid.

When I finally was able to call Jim, I sobbed as I told him what had happened. I was so relieved that the Lord had answered our prayers. I don't think he really believed me until he came into town and saw those darling babies lying in the bed next to Peggy!

I stayed with Peggy and the twins for seven hours. I didn't want to leave until I was sure they were all okay. When I came home, I was exhausted but couldn't sleep. This was the most awesome event in my life! I gathered my obstetrical books to read about twins. Statistically, one baby stood a greater chance of being breech, and hemorrhaging is the biggest threat to the mother. I'm glad I did my reading afterwards.

*Thank you, Lord, for using a nightmare, so we would know how to pray. You knew all the time that Peggy was carrying twins. I know, after this experience, I can trust you for anything!*

*"For thou hast possessed my inward parts; thou hast covered me in my mother's womb. I will praise thee; for I am fearfully and wonderfully made. Marvelous are thy works, and that my soul knoweth right well. My substance was not hidden from thee, when I was made in secret, and intricately woven in the lowest parts of the earth. Thine eyes did see my substance, yet being unformed; and in thy book all my*

*members were written, which in continuance were fashioned, when as yet there was none of them. How precious also are thy thoughts unto me, O. God!"* (Psalm 139:13-17).

Grace and Sarah might have been a surprise to us, but they never were to God!

Chapter Ten

Acknowledging Him as Guide

*"Teach me thy way, O Lord, and lead me in a plain path..."*
(Psalm 27:11a).

### West Palm Beach, Florida   1971

Sitting in the car that August afternoon, I shuddered as I considered my bold, somewhat impulsive statement a few minutes before. "I'll be back in two hours with an apartment for Sally and Ellen."

The remark was made to refute a fellow teacher at the Christian school where I was going to teach Home Economics. We were attending teachers' meetings before the fall semester. Jack, a part-time realtor, was doing a good job of discouraging two young ladies who were on their first teaching assignment.

"Apartments are scarce in this area and very expensive," Jack warned the girls. "Besides, neither of you owns a car. That really limits your possibilities since there's no public transportation."

Just the night before, Jim and I had prayed with Sally. "Lord, help Sally and Ellen find an apartment. We'd like one exactly suited to their needs - reasonable rent, within walking distance to the school, air-conditioned, with two bedrooms."

As I listened to Jack's negative report, my mind quickly jumped back to that prayer and I took a step of ......was it faith, or presumption? Now, alone in my car, I prayed again, "Lord, I need your HELP!"

My first thought was to do the logical thing. I headed for an area where many apartments were located, hoping that I'd find one. If I did, perhaps the girls could find a ride or buy a car. *After all*, I reasoned, *August isn't the tourist season and two hours will give me plenty of time to find something.*

Almost one hour and forty-five minutes later, my optimism had fled. I had knocked on so many apartment office doors and heard the same response, "Sorry, no vacancies." Dejected, I headed back to the school ready to admit defeat. My allotted time was fast coming to a close, and I had a training session to attend. I had almost turned into the school parking lot when a Bible verse interrupted my somber train of thought.

*"Trust in the Lord with all thine heart and lean not unto thine own understanding. In all thy ways acknowledge him, and he shall direct thy paths"* (Proverbs 3:5,6).

*I'm sorry, Lord. I asked for your help and instead of waiting for you to speak, I allowed my human intellect to direct my path. No wonder my efforts were fruitless. Please forgive me and direct me to where you know there is an available apartment."*

**"Continue up the street and turn left."**

*Is that you, Lord? That would lead to a business district. There are no apartments there. Whoops, here I go, reasoning again. I'm sorry; I'll obey.*

Past the school driveway I drove, having no idea of my destination. Now my spiritual ears were turned on, and I was a sheep listening for the shepherd's voice.

**"Turn right at the corner."**

The clock was ticking away. I had fifteen minutes left before my scheduled meeting. I turned right at the corner onto the busy thoroughfare.

Another nudge pervaded my mind. **"Turn left."**

Obediently turning left onto a small street that I had never noticed before, I found myself in an area lined with duplex apartments. Then I saw exactly what I had hoped for earlier. There in a window was a sign - TWO BEDROOM APARTMENT FOR RENT.

*Hallelujah!*

Confident now, I knocked on the door. When the landlady answered, I somewhat boldly informed her, "I've come for the apartment."

"For you and your husband?"

"No, for two single female teachers at the Christian school down the road."

"Oh no, that isn't possible," she responded. "Didn't you read the newspaper ad? It said MARRIED COUPLE ONLY."

"I'm sorry, I didn't. I wouldn't have bothered you if I had known." I looked at my watch, knowing I had less than ten minutes left. Almost pleadingly, I continued, "We prayed for the perfect apartment for the girls, and this seemed to be the answer."

The lady's face lit up, and she laughed, "Well, I'm a Christian too. If you prayed about it, I'm not one to interfere with God's answer. I'll be happy to rent it to them!"

Jubilantly, I floated back to school in time to make my announcement, "I found the perfect apartment. I mean, THE LORD found the perfect apartment! It has two bedrooms, air-conditioning, reasonable rent, and it's right across the highway!"

This event greatly encouraged me to learn to listen for the Lord's voice and *to follow where He leads.*

*"My sheep hear my voice, and I know them, and they follow me"* (John 10:27).

As I gradually learned to eliminate some of the noisy distractions from my life, many times I could hear that still, small voice of the Lord when He spoke. He doesn't shout to be heard, I found. He just waits for me to get quiet and listen.

Getting quiet meant focusing on His Word more than on my human intellect or reasoning. It meant filling my mind with the things I was told to think about in **Philippians 4:8**; things that are true, pure, lovely, virtuous, and praiseworthy. In **Proverbs 4:23**, I read, "*Keep thy heart with all diligence, for out of it are the issues of life."* To truly *"be in the world, but not of it"* became the deepest longing of my heart. I wanted to hear His voice and be led by His Spirit. The more I obeyed Him, the clearer His voice has become over the years.

### Wisconsin  July 4, 1974

In the aftermath of the academy trauma, Jim sent the children and me to Minnesota with my friend Beb. We picnicked our meals on the way there. The six children, riding in the cramped quarters of the pickup camper shell, needed time to exercise.

We Floridians were accustomed to a blistering hot Fourth of July. This day was more like our January weather! It was cool, cloudy, and blustery.

"A hot lunch would sure taste good," commented Beb. "I wonder what's wrong with our Coleman stove? It wouldn't light for anything last night. Oh well, cold sandwiches will have to do!"

I was doing the driving as lunch time neared and was thinking about the problem with the stove. *"A hot lunch would be enjoyable,"* I silently agreed.

**"Up ahead there's a roadside park. Pull off and ask the man in the car next to you to fix the stove."**

I glanced over at Beb. She was quietly gazing out the window. She obviously hadn't said anything. I didn't comment.

This was my first time in Wisconsin, so I had no idea of what was up ahead. In less than five minutes, I saw a sign that sent shivers down my spine, ROADSIDE PARK AHEAD.

Telling Beb what I thought the Lord instructed, I obediently pulled into the park area and the first available parking spot. There were empty cars on either side of us, but no man around that we could see.

While the children explored a nearby nature trail, we unloaded our picnic supplies. We both held our breath as we saw a man meandering toward us. He approached the car to the left of us and opened the door. I summoned up my courage and asked, "Can you fix a Coleman stove?"

Without hesitation, he took our stove to a nearby picnic table and replied, "I'll bet you've done what I did the first time I used one of these." With that, he tightened something, primed the pump, and lit the stove. "Enjoy your lunch," he cheerfully said as he walked to his car and drove away.

Beb and I stood in awe as we watched him leave. *Was the man a real person or an angel?* I reflected. It really didn't matter. The Lord saw our need and met it. Our hot lunch was ready when the children returned from their walk.

**Palm Beach Gardens, Florida   1975**
Sometimes this guidance comes over such seemingly trivial matters that I can only be assured of God's love for me. The things that concern me seem to touch His heart, too. Isn't that how a loving father should be with his children?

One time my dad was in the hospital and I went to visit him. When I got out of the car in the parking lot, a sudden downpour sent me scrambling. My purse slipped from my hand, dumping all its contents on the wet pavement. I hurriedly snatched up the sodden mess, threw it back in my purse, and ran to visit Dad.

I didn't think any more about the incident until that evening. We were at a Bible study and I reached in my purse for my gold Cross pen to take notes. It wasn't there. Discouraged, I remembered dropping my purse in the parking lot at the hospital. I was upset. The pen was a special anniversary gift from Jim, and I regretted losing it.

Early the next morning, I called the hospital, hoping someone had found it and had turned it in. No such luck.

Then I heard it - that still, small voice, **"Go to the hospital parking lot. NOW!"** With the thought, a picture came into my mind. I saw the parking lot at the hospital and my gold pen lying near a curb bumper next to a telephone pole.

My human reasoning seemed to say, *You aren't even dressed yet. Wait until you go to visit Dad this afternoon.* In the natural, that made more sense, but I was trying to walk in the Spirit. The Lord said, "Go now," so I got dressed and drove to the hospital parking lot. Driving directly to the spot I had seen in my mind, I parked the car. Yes, there's the telephone pole! Next to the pole was a concrete curb bumper, and lying in full view against it was my pen. By visiting hours, it surely would have been gone.

**West Palm Beach, Florida    January 1975**
Hearing little instructions from the Lord is as important as hearing big ones. On my path of life, some events have made me very aware of the importance of tuning in to His voice.

One particular day, I met a special friend to shop for fabric for her wedding gown. My whole focus of attention was on the kind of material we'd buy and the design I planned to recommend. I was happy for her and blessed that I would sew her gown. We shopped and chatted for hours. After we finally made all our purchases, we wearily went our separate ways.

Driving out of the shopping center, I was still thinking about the wedding gown when another thought interrupted me. **Turn down this street.**

I turned down the street to my right, thinking that it would probably be a shortcut out of the heavy traffic. The Lord knew I was tired, so I thought He was just being kind.

He was being kind, but not necessarily to me at the moment.

There was a nursing home on this side street. As I passed it, I caught sight of an older woman who stumbled and fell in the yard. She didn't try to get up. *Maybe she had a heart attack.* Quickly I pulled over to the curb and ran to assist her, assuming that she was one of the residents out for a stroll.

Shocked, I found a very inebriated older woman lying there. She didn't belong to the nursing home at all. As I helped her to her feet, she told me that her name was Florence. She then proceeded to relate a jumbled story. Piecing together her tale, I realized that a man she had met invited her to lunch at a restaurant in the area. He offered her a cocktail before lunch, and then another, and another. Suddenly feeling sick and lightheaded, she excused herself to go out for some fresh air. The next thing she knew, she was here on the ground.

I offered to drive her back to the restaurant, but she pleaded with me to take her home. Not being sure what to do, I agreed and hoped she really remembered where she lived. She directed me to a large retirement community several miles away. All the way there, she kept calling me her "angel" and offering me money and some of her jewelry. She was so intoxicated that I simply said, "Florence, I don't want anything you can give me. The Lord had me there at the right time to help you. After you're sober, I want to get together. There's something I want to give you."

Entering her attractive apartment, I helped her into bed and left my name and phone number on the table. I locked the door and left.

*What a strange circumstance. Lord, you brought Florence into my life. Please let me lead her to you. You loved her enough to protect her from someone who would have taken advantage of her. Help her to understand that.*

Later that evening, Florence called. By now she was feeling embarrassed at her behavior. "I never drink," she informed me. "My husband recently died, and I'm so lonely. When I was invited out to lunch, I was glad to have some companionship. Lou insisted that I have a drink to celebrate his birthday with him, and I did. He kept drinking, and so did I. I don't know why I was so foolish. You were sent as my angel, and I want to do something for you."

"Florence, I'm a Christian, and I want an opportunity to share Jesus with you. That's what you can do for me." I answered.

A few days later, she invited me to her apartment for a visit. Although a churchgoer, she had never considered a personal relationship with Christ. I knew I had a distinct advantage. "Florence, I'm not an angel, but God certainly loved you enough to bring me into your life to share His love with you. He's the one who deserves your praise, not me."

We continued to meet for the next several weeks. At each session, I shared the Bible and left Christian books for her to read. On February 10, Florence knelt with me on her living room floor to repent of her sins. Florence didn't have children or family. Since her husband died, she had such an emptiness in her life. Now Jesus could begin to fill all the voids in her life.

Soon afterward, she joined our church and was surrounded by the love of her brothers and sisters in Christ.

One Sunday morning, Florence asked Jim to baptize her. That was such a day of rejoicing for everyone present. A short time later, Florence had a heart attack and died. She was ready to be with Jesus.

*Thank you for guiding me to that nursing home yard, Lord. Help me to always listen to your voice.*

### Highland, New York  1984

Jim had a talk with Bonnie one afternoon. "You know, I've been thinking that there was a real value to arranged marriages in Bible times," he told her. "After all, parents can evaluate a young person a lot more realistically than another young person who may be blinded by physical attraction or infatuation."

A few days later, Bonnie returned to her dad with a request. "Dad, I've been thinking a lot about what you said about arranged marriages, and I see the wisdom in it. Would you find me a husband? Then, with a concerned look on her face, she asked, "Can I approve of your choice?"

Jim assured her that she certainly could. Then, shocked by the absolute sincerity of his daughter's request, Jim hurriedly went into the bedroom, fell to his knees, and prayed, "Oh, Lord, did you hear what Bonnie just asked me to do?" He went on to pray specifically that the Lord would find the young man Bonnie was to marry, turn him around, and cause his path to cross hers.

One Sunday afternoon, a group of people from our church attended a performance of a Christian drama team in a nearby town. Bonnie and I had other plans for that afternoon, so we weren't able to join them.

Several people, including Jim, were impressed by one particular young actor named Chris. A few women from our congregation told Bonnie about him. Whoever "Chris" was, he became a means of teasing Bonnie, although she had never seen or met him.

Months later, Bonnie was invited to join this particular drama team. She attended her first rehearsal held in a Christian coffee house. Overhearing some of the team members talking, she realized that the "mystery man," Chris, had moved to New Jersey.

"Dad, if that Chris is the man God has for me, you'll have to pray him back. He moved to New Jersey!" Bonnie reported when she arrived home.

More time elapsed, and Bonnie was thoroughly enjoying acting. She was learning how effectively scriptural truth can be presented through drama.

One night when Bonnie attended a rehearsal, a new young man was there to practice. After rehearsal, she became acquainted over a cup of coffee. To her amazement, she discovered that she was actually sitting across the table from the Chris! He had recently moved back to New York and rejoined the drama team. More to her amazement, he was nice, and nice-looking to boot! After all the months of teasing, she wasn't expecting to ever meet him or to like him if she did.

Chris invited her to go to the county fair with him. We had a friend's two young teen-age daughters staying with us that night. Bonnie told Chris that she'd be happy to go to the fair if our house-guests could go, too. Poor guy! He agreed to take all three girls.

Chris and Bonnie soon began to date seriously, with our approval. It was very difficult for us not to be overprotective after the trauma we had been through with Loryn. We had no confidence in our judgment, but we knew that it was imperative to give our fears to God. After all, Jim had prayed for Bonnie's future husband, and we had to trust the Lord with the results of this relationship. Only God knew the path of life for each child, and we could only relinquish our control.

I realized Jim had successfully arrived at this point when Chris casually asked one day, "What do you think about Bonnie and me?"

"I think you're God's man for her," was Jim's succinct reply. Chris later admitted to his shock over this answer. He had expected something like, "You're a nice guy!" Marriage wasn't even in his mind yet.

The relationship gained momentum, however, and before long, Chris approached Jim for permission to marry Bonnie. By this time, he had spent many evenings at our dinner table and he had become like one of the family. He willingly submitted to our close scrutiny, knowing what a difficult time we had had before. We felt secure that Chris was indeed the answer to Jim's prayers, and permission to marry our youngest daughter was freely granted.

The details were interesting when Jim and Chris compared notes. At the very time Jim started praying for Bonnie's future husband to be turned around and headed in her direction, the circumstances in Chris's life changed dramatically. These changes culminated in his moving back to our area and rejoining the drama team.

On September 28, 1985, Chris and Bonnie were married.

### Huntsville, Arkansas 1991

We heard a preacher tell a story about a horse a man owned. "Does God heal horses?" the man asked.

"If you have the faith to believe, he does," was the preacher's reply.

"Well, my prized horse is very sick, and the vet wants to euthanize it. Would you pray for my horse to get well?"

The preacher went on to say to the audience, "If you don't believe God heals horses, let your horse die. This horse was healed, and the grateful owner presented me with a huge portrait of him. It's on my study wall as a reminder that God cares about our animals."

The memory of that story was brought to our minds when our dog disappeared. A pedigreed Irish Setter, Ginger was also Joshua's Christmas gift and his companion on many adventures in the woods. She was special to me because she replaced our first Ginger, who was run over by a car in New York. Now she had been missing for two days.

We prayed for her to come home, but on the third day Jim felt urged to pray a specific prayer, "Lord Jesus, help Ginger get loose."

"Why did you pray for her to get loose?" I asked.

Jim informed us that he had a strong impression that she was tied up somewhere. Guidance from the Holy Spirit covers a multitude of concerns in our lives if we're listening. His guidance reveals His will.

*"And this is the confidence that we have in him, that, if we ask anything according to his will, he hears us; And if we know that he hear us, whatever we ask, we know that we have the petitions that we desire of him"* (I John 5:14,15).

Several hours after Jim's prayer, the phone rang. "Is Ginger missing?" asked our veterinarian's receptionist.

"Yes, do you know where she is?"

"This is a really bizarre story," she replied. "An elderly lady just called from Combs about an Irish Setter that turned up at her house yesterday. The dog came up on her porch and kept running back and forth to the road. She said it seemed that the dog wanted her to follow it, but it was a strange dog so she stayed inside. She noticed that the dog was without a collar. Anyway, the dog finally disappeared. This morning, the dog reappeared and dropped something in front of her door. Curious, she looked to see what it was and found a dog collar with our rabies tag on it. The heavy leather collar had been slit clean through. Of course the rabies tag had our phone number on it, so she called."

"Where in the world is Combs?" I asked.

"It's way south of Kingston. We think Ginger was stolen and must have gotten loose from her captors. We got a call warning us of an illegal "dog swap," soon to take place in the area. The police told us to warn our clients that thieves steal large dogs and sell them for laboratory use."

I wrote down the directions to the lady's house and thanked her. Josh and I jumped in the van and headed out toward Combs. It was 25 miles away over several mountains.

When we drove into the driveway, no one would have doubted our ownership of Ginger. She was jubilantly dancing all over the yard when she saw us drive in. Her coat was free from burrs, and her energy level made it apparent that she hadn't traveled 25 miles through the mountainous terrain on foot. We thanked the lady for calling the vet and backtracked to our home.

"Ginger's just like Lassie! She's so smart!" was the excited exclamation from everyone who heard the story.

We knew better. We love our dog, but we have a more realistic view of her limited intelligence. God heard Jim's prayer that she "get loose" and enabled her to do the rest.

If you don't believe the Lord finds dogs, let your dog stay lost!

**Virginia  May 1993**

We were increasingly aware that we needed some answers to Joshua's distractibility. As he grew older, I expected the problem to improve, not worsen. Many times in recent months I was convinced that we were going backwards. He seemed to jump from thing to thing to thing, with no focus. Jobs were left undone or half-finished. Left to himself, in the space of fifteen minutes, he could play the piano, shoot baskets, throw the baseball, and weed a few weeds in the garden. His flitting around, not accomplishing any task, made me very agitated. Home-schooling allowed me to be painfully aware of his problem. I was also aware of my growing impatience. I knew in my heart that Josh had a desire to please us and God. His motives were never in question. I had been praying for guidance, for both of us. Nagging was certainly not a solution, but I was doing it more and more. Many times we were both discouraged.

Fulfilling a promise to my mother, I flew to Florida, drove her to Rhode Island, and visited her ailing sister. As we traveled, there were times our conversation was very limited. The whole focus of my life was Jesus, and I couldn't talk to Mom about Him. We didn't have a lot in common. We read different kinds of books and had different political and social views. Consequently, I spent many quiet hours silently praying for an answer to my current need. I wanted to help Josh focus, but my past efforts seemed futile.

Christian radio stations were on the "no-no" list as we traveled, but one morning a familiar voice captured my attention. I was flipping the dial looking for some acceptable music. *Dr. Dobson!* ("Focus on the Family") Glancing at Mom, she seemed to be snoozing. *Maybe I can listen for a few minutes with the volume low.*

It was a talk show that morning with a panel discussion on Attention Deficit Hyperactivity Disorder (ADHD). The people discussing their children were describing Joshua. Most children with this disorder are bright but have difficulty focusing. Some of the symptoms fit Josh to a "T"; others didn't. Enough did, that I was excited when a book was suggested, The Hyperactive Child, by Dr. Grant Martin. Two more programs on the subject of ADHD were to follow on subsequent days. I knew my chances of listening to them was remote.

"SanDee, would you please stop at the next rest area."

I had a wonderful idea. *While Mom's in the restroom, I'll call Jim.* Mom headed up the path to the restroom, and I hurriedly dashed to a pay phone. "Jim, be sure to tune in to "Focus on the Family" this morning! Order the tapes from today and the next two days and the book by Dr. Martin. I think the Lord gave us an answer for Joshua!" (My poor husband was used to my whims by now, but I was sure he'd agree with me after hearing the program.)  "I love you! Bye!"

That was the only time in the three weeks Mom and I were traveling that I got away with listening to Christian radio. It was the only time I needed an answer.

The book by Dr. Martin gave us so much hope. In it, not only were symptoms described but concrete solutions for training such a child to focus. We were able to glean answers suited to Joshua's needs. When we discussed our plan, he also was relieved to have some answers. With his willing cooperation and our understanding, the frustration level has noticeably diminished.

Someone might call my tuning into a radio station in Virginia at that particular time on that particular day, coincidence. I call it an answer to prayer for guidance.

## Chapter Eleven

## Acknowledging Him as Travel Agent

*"The steps of a good man are ordered by the Lord: and he delighteth in his way"* (Psalm 37:23).

### Nassau, Bahamas 1974

There's a song we used to sing in a church we attended. The first line is meaningful to me, "Where He leads me, I will follow." Instead of making our own travel plans, we were learning to let the Lord plan our trips for us. That way, we could be used by Him in places we may otherwise never visit because of either a of lack of desire, or more than likely, a lack of funds.

A pastor friend was burdened for his daughter and son-in-law who lived in Nassau. One day as we were visiting him, he received a long-distance phone call from his daughter. His son-in-law, having once served the Lord, had fallen away. Their marriage was suffering because of his unwise decision and resulting actions. Our friend was very troubled, and my heart ached for him.

We had become acquainted with his daughter on her visits to her parents, and we dearly loved her. "How much would it cost for Jim and me to fly to Nassau? We would love to have an opportunity to encourage Ruth and possibly minister to DeWitt, if he'd listen to us."

"You mean you'd really take the time to do that? If you would, I'd be happy to pay your fare. Sometimes, someone outside of the family is able to be more objective. I know Ruth, at least, would appreciate the visit. She desperately needs encouragement."

Soon we were in a small plane flying to Nassau. Once there, our friend had arranged for us to stay with a team of young Christians who were distributing literature on the island and preaching the gospel. The fellowship with them was a blessing. Arrangements were made for us to spend a full day with Ruth and DeWitt. Having been born and raised in Nassau, DeWitt was enthusiastic about showing us the island. It's always more interesting to see a country through the eyes of a native, and we were very interested in learning about the culture of the people.

DeWitt took us on a tour to show us his homeland. Our genuine interest seemed to help him relax with us. Most of the day was spent in lighthearted banter. We prayed for an opening for serious conversation and a sensitivity to recognize it.

A couple of incidents along the way convinced us that we were being tested. Stopping along a dock, we watched as conch shells were being emptied of their slimy inhabitants. "We're going to have conch salad for dinner tonight," DeWitt informed us. "We eat it RAW!" DeWitt watched my face as he emphasized RAW, probably convinced that I'd react to the idea.

"I love to try new dishes!" I replied without flinching. *Lord, help my stomach to agree!*

Later that day, he proudly took us to the gambling casino on Paradise Island. As Christians, we could have refused to go in, but even Jesus ate with publicans and sinners! Refusing might have shut a door. By the end of the day, DeWitt appeared to trust us, and an opening finally came to talk to him about his deep spiritual need. Ruth and I had some quality time alone to discuss her role as a wife in a difficult situation. We reviewed many scriptures together and had time to pray.

We really had enjoyed the day. We watched as little boys dove after coins in the sparkling turquoise water near the cruise ship docks. Driving on the left side of the road was a new and strange experience for us. The sugar-sand beaches, colorful market places, and the wide-eyed, delightfully curious, barefoot children gave us a flavor of another culture.

DeWitt wasn't kidding about the raw conch salad! He personally prepared it for us that evening. The pieces of conch were rubbery, but they were in such a hot sauce that we really couldn't taste anything else. Our stomachs passed the test!

While on the island, Jim had the opportunity to speak to an assembly of children at a Christian school. That seemed incidental to what we thought was the real purpose for our visit to the school. We spent time with the principal and vice-principal, sharing our testimony as an encouragement to them. Many times in his teaching, Jim shares a truth he learned. "God is an economist. He uses each willing vessel and each situation as many ways as possible." We were already in Nassau on one mission, so the Lord optimized our visits with DeWitt and Ruth, the school, and our time with the team who hosted us.

**Western United States    July - August 1976**

Early in 1975, Jim had a wonderful idea. "Let's save for a trip to Europe in 1976 for the whole family. Loryn will be graduating from high school next year, and it might be our last family vacation together. We have a small insurance policy coming due, and we can use those funds supplemented by what we can save in the next year or so."

We were excited at the prospect and asked the Lord to bless our plans. We didn't think to ask about **His plans**, and the stark reality of that fact became apparent as the year progressed. Our savings began to dwindle, instead of flourish. The pump to our well broke; the car needed expensive repairs; the roof leaked. *"......he that earneth wages earneth wages to put it into a bag with holes. Thus saith the Lord of hosts: Consider your ways"* (Haggai 1:6b,7). We certainly felt as though our vacation savings was in a bag with holes in it!

"Maybe we aren't supposed to go to Europe." I finally voiced a nagging doubt to Jim.

"Let's pray about it. Something isn't right, that's for sure. We were so excited about our plans that we never really asked the Lord if He agreed with them." Right then and there, Jim bowed his head and prayed, "Lord Jesus, we're willing to chuck our plans if you want us to go somewhere else, or nowhere at all. Please show us clearly."

In a short time, we became aware of all the wonderful offers from car rental businesses, motels, and recreation areas for the summer of 1976. It was the bicentennial year, and Americans were being encouraged to see their own country. That idea suddenly felt so right. Perhaps this was the Lord's will for us. We began to pray in that direction, knowing we couldn't take much of a vacation with our present savings.

Soon we were involved in one of God's economist episodes. We began to pray about direction for our steps, and He had so much more in mind.

My dressmaking business had increased over the years. As we worked together, the income paid for not only our four children's tuition but also that of my friend Dorothy's four children. We soon had more work than we could comfortably handle, and another friend began to work with us part-time. My little sewing room simply couldn't accommodate all of us, and we overflowed into our adjoining bedroom. The deep shag carpeting made a wonderful hiding place for dropped pins. Jim's bare feet, to my chagrin, found every one!

A shop became available in a lovely location near the beach, and it seemed to be the solution. The rent was reasonable, and there was adequate room for a few employees, a fitting room, and a reception area. We decided to rent it. The shop would open two hours after Jim and the children left for school and would close before they came home. We wouldn't open on weekends or in the summer. Most of my customers were winter visitors to Florida, so that would be perfect. It also would keep me from heading to my sewing room in the evening to work when I had something I couldn't get out of my mind.

The shop was blessed, but after three years, I was tired. The responsibility of all the cutting and fitting fell on me, and many customers were very demanding. Jim and I toyed with the idea of selling the shop.

While the idea was in seed form, the Lord watered it, and we watched it grow. I received a phone call from a woman with a foreign accent asking if I needed help. I didn't, but took her name and phone number. A few days later, I had an interesting thought, *Call and ask the woman who phoned if she wants to buy the business*. In a short time, the business was sold to Beya and her husband, Moncef. The proceeds were added to our vacation fund.

The rest of the story is a tribute to God's love and His ability to economize by doing several things instead of one.

Beya and Moncef were Moslems from Tunisia, North Africa. We were able to lead them to Jesus and see them become a part of our church. Their souls were far more important to the Lord than the selling of a shop or a vacation.

God wasn't through yet. The landlord of the building where the shop was located recommended an attorney to draw up a sales contract. The lawyer, in discussing the sale of the shop, asked me how it had come about. Joyfully, I shared how I thought the Lord had Beya call, and I related the events that followed. My story raised the lawyer's curiosity. I ended up spending an hour sharing my testimony with him, as he listened with rapt attention. When I finished talking, he said, "You touched on every area of need in my life!"

"What do you mean?" I asked in amazement.

"I have a friend with cancer, a son who is engaged to a Jewish girl, and another son with eye problems!"

As I prepared to leave his office, I inquired about the fee for the legal work he was to do for us. "Nothing." he replied. "I couldn't charge you after this last hour."

When Jesus fed the multitudes, He used two little fish and five small loaves of bread. Now that we had lined up with His will for our trip, He used an Arab couple and a lawyer to multiply our money.

By the time we left for vacation, we were able to rent a brand new, nine-passenger stationwagon instead of driving our less dependable vehicle. Because of the bicentennial deals, there was only a weekly fee, no limits, and no mileage charge.

We took a notebook along on the trip for a journal. Every evening when we stopped for the night, we each wrote down a sentence or two about our impressions for the day.

### New Orleans, Louisiana July 5, 1976

Ten-year-old Bonnie wrote, "Today in the French Quarter there were a lot of evil things, but we still praised the Lord for seeing a Christian bookstore, and we hoped the books would help someone."

### Dallas, Texas July 7, 1976

Twelve-year-old Jeff wrote, "Today I was impressed by the road in Dallas because the road just ran in a circle around it, and you got off wherever you wanted."

### Carlsbad Caverns, New Mexico  July 10, 1976

Fourteen-year-old Tim wrote, "Today was probably the best and most enjoyable day so far. The caves really impressed me. I liked looking down into the deep caverns. What I liked most about the caves were the beautiful formations all around. I also climbed a 200 or 250 foot high hill!"

### Arizona desert  July 11, 1976

Sixteen-year-old Loryn wrote, "I enjoyed the dust storm because it was new and exciting. I also enjoyed laughing at a man who was rude in Howard Johnson's. (He couldn't believe a cup of coffee was 30 whole cents)"

### Sun City, Arizona  July 12, 1976

Jim wrote, "Today's impression was the austere desert vegetation, particularly in the lawns (?) seen in Sun City. Front yards have green gravel and cactus, back yards have brown gravel and cactus just about the extreme opposite of the Garden of Eden."

### Sedona, Arizona and Grand Canyon, Arizona  July 13, 1976

I wrote, "Climbing in the red rock near Sedona was nice - beautiful scenery. The Grand Canyon at sunset turned out to be the Grand Canyon in a thunderstorm - an awesome and scary experience. No pictures or words could describe what we saw tonight."

Every day brought other awesome sights of God's handiwork. We marvelled together at the amazing variety of animals in the San Diego Zoo. None of us had ever seen the big-nosed proboscis monkey, and we stood laughing together at God's sense of humor.

Jim commented in southern California that the Pacific Ocean looked a lot like the Atlantic, except it's on the wrong side of the road!

God's creativity continued to impress us as we stood gaping at the giant sequoia trees in the Sequoia National Park and the immense rock formations and Bridal Veil Falls in Yosemite.

Chinatown in San Francisco afforded us an opportunity to eat Chinese food for lunch and to experience a different culture right in our own country. Jeff wrote that he was impressed by the low prices.

By the time we reached the route along the ocean north of San Francisco, Jim changed his mind about the Pacific looking like the Atlantic. He wrote, "The impression today was the beauty of the coastline - the rocks on the coast and the hills right across the road. At times, the roadway rose to several hundred feet, looking down sheer rock cliffs to the pounding surf of the Pacific -- quite a beautiful contrast to Florida's flat beaches. Praise God for His variety!"

On July 26, we saw snow. Our Florida-born kids were ecstatic! Every one of us wrote comments about the snow at Crater Lake, Oregon, that day. Jeff wrote, "Today was the funnest!!! We first saw a small patch of snow and were very excited! But later, after seeing the beautiful crater lake, we slid down a very big hill of snow and that was super fun !!!!"

Mt. Rainier gave me an opportunity to be a hero in my kids' eyes. The snow on the glaciers was deep. Tim found a cardboard box and flattened it to make a sled. He convinced me that I could climb the glacier and join the children's sledding excursion. Halfway up the dizzying incline, I was tempted to change my mind, but Tim kept egging me on, "You can do it Mom!  Come on, you're doing great!" So up I climbed until Tim decided it was high enough for me, and he handed me the piece of cardboard. Positioning myself firmly in the center of it, I held on for dear life. Shoving off with a whoosh, I went flying down the hill. About halfway down, the "sled" involuntarily turned me around and I fell backward. The rest of the way down, my head pretended that it was a snowplow! I wasn't hurt, but as I reached a level place and stopped, I was laughing so hard I couldn't get up. From their vantage point, the kids on the hill remembered a recent movie about a skier who was paralyzed in a fall, and they were frightened. Scurrying down, they found me with nothing more injured than my pride, and we had a good laugh.

Jim wrote in the journal that day, "The **five** children had fun sliding down steep slopes of snow on either scraps of cardboard or their bare britches. Frostbite in late July sounds unlikely, but today it sounds more plausible." I wrote that sliding on the snow was reminiscent of my childhood!

Many times we saw God's provision as we traveled. The entries on July 29 found all of us mentioning the provision of a motel that night in Missoula, Montana. We got into town late, without reservations. On our first pass through town, every motel had a NO VACANCY sign. Jeff best describes what happened, "Today we couldn't find a motel and we saw NO on a motel. Then we prayed and came back and it was YES; there were beds for all of us and an elevator." Someone with reservations hadn't shown up, and as we turned around and came back through town, the NO became YES, just when we needed it! Thank you, Lord.

Yellowstone National Park gave Tim the impression of being on another planet. Bonnie's entry said, "I liked seeing Old Faithful blow his top."

On August 1, we were in Grand Teton National Park, Wyoming. I wrote, "Years ago, I saw a large photograph of the Grand Tetons, and I was impressed by the beauty. God is so good to allow us to see these beautiful mountains - no picture could adequately capture their majesty."

August 2 was the fateful day in Jackson Hole, Wyoming. As traumatic as it was for Jim and me, thinking our boys were lost, Tim's entry in the journal is amusing. "I enjoyed looking in the shops in Jackson Hole, but mostly, I enjoyed climbing a mountain to the top. We saw a lot of bones on the mountain."

From Salt Lake City, Utah, we headed home to Florida. We had traveled through 16 states in our 40-day vacation and had covered 10,134 trouble-free miles!

With this trip and other vacations in the past, we had seen every state, with the exception of Maine, Alaska, and Hawaii. We praised God for the privilege of living in America, the beautiful. We had now seen it from sea to shining sea.

When God closed the door to a European trip, Jim and I recognized that it was His plan to teach the children an appreciation for the beauty of our own country. We were so glad He did.

## Israel - The Feast of Tabernacles   October, 1984

Sally called from Buffalo, New York, on a summer day. She could hardly contain her excitement. "I'm going to Israel with a church group in October! Why don't you and Jim go, too?" Sally had remained our friend ever since the first day we met her at the academy in Florida. She had taught two of our children and had even lived with us for eighteen months. Eventually, we had gone our separate ways, but here we were, all in New York state.

Within a few days, our friend Roger, pastor of a Messianic congregation in Queens, New York, called with the same invitation. "I'm going to Israel in October. Would you like to go?" Ironically, he was going on the same tour as Sally.

That day I was flying to Florida for the weekend to attend the wedding of a friend's daughter. On the way to the airport, I told Jim, "I never really even wanted to go to Israel until now. This year, teaching the women's Bible study about Israel has put such a longing in my heart to actually see the Holy Land. Now that Sally and Roger are going, I want us to go, too. Can we agree to pray for the money?" Driving along, Jim prayed that if the Lord wanted us to go to Israel in October, He'd provide the way.

Since I was going to be in Florida for only a couple of days, my mom and dad drove from their home in Deerfield Beach to West Palm Beach to see me that afternoon. They also wanted to take me to the nursing home to see Jim's mother while I was in the area. On the way, Mom asked, "Would you like to go to Israel?"

Assuming it was just a conversational question, I replied, "I really would."

Dad immediately asked, "When?"

"In October."

"Make plans. We'll pay for you and Jim to go."

My Jewish parents, who never had any desire to go to Israel, were now offering to send us on the very day we prayed for God to provide the way. That was not a coincidence; it was a miracle!

I got to a phone as soon as I possibly could. "Jim, find out what we have to do to make reservations and get passports! We're going to

Israel! God answered the prayer you prayed this morning." I was so excited that it took me a few minutes to settle down and make sense.

The trip was a highlight of our lives. We arrived in Tel Aviv and journeyed to Jerusalem by bus. The closer we got, the more we had the sense of "coming home." It was evening by the time we settled into our hotel. As soon as we could slip away, Jim and I headed hand in hand toward the wall of the old city. It was a profound spiritual experience. So many times we had sat bored through other people's slides and talks about their trips to Israel. Now we understood the enthusiasm they had exhibited. We were in Jerusalem - God's city.

*"But I have chosen Jerusalem, that my name might be there..."* (II Chronicles 6:6).

*"In Jerusalem shall my name be forever"* (II Chronicles 33:4).

The days were filled with splendor. We attended the Feast of Tabernacles Celebration, a Christian conference in Jerusalem. Six thousand Christians from all over the world were there. Every day brought special events.

One afternoon we all gathered on the top of the Mount of Olives. Many people carried beautiful banners with Old Testament verses on them. Down the hill we marched singing praises to our God as we went through the Kidron Valley, past the Eastern Gate, and on to the Western (wailing) Wall. We sang "We're Marching to Zion," and we really were!

Another time, we were bused to a field in Qumran, facing the caves where the Dead Sea Scrolls had been found by a young goatherd in 1947. Each person was given a box lunch, and we sat on blankets watching the sun set as we ate. There was a blessed time of worship together before we returned to the buses for our trek back to Jerusalem.

For me as a Jewish Christian, there were both rejoicing and grieving times. A Russian Jewish immigrant spoke one morning and showed a film of present-day concentration camps in the Soviet Union. The movie looked as though it were taken by someone with a very unsteady camera hand. A few minutes into the film, a question was posed to the viewer, "Does the shakiness of the pictures you're seeing bother you? If it does, know that it was taken at the possible expense of the filmer's life." The narrator went on to explain that the camera was hidden in a suitcase equipped with a tiny hole for the lens to be able to capture the atrocities. One particular mine entrance was filmed. Many people, Christians and Jews, were arrested for falsified reasons and were sent into this mine. Thousands went in; few came out.

The gentleman showing the film then told of his experiences. He was placed in a box in Siberia in freezing weather. The box was so small that he remained in a crouched position, unable to stand erect. Both of his legs froze and eventually had to be amputated. He considered himself one of the lucky ones - he lived to fulfill the dream of any religious Jew - he was allowed to come to the Jewish homeland, Israel.

That same day, we visited the Holocaust Museum in Jerusalem. A long walkway to the museum was planted with trees honoring the "righteous Gentiles" who helped the Jews during Hitler's regime. The most famous to me was Corrie ten Boom, but I was blessed to discover there were so many more.

The purpose of the museum was a reminder to the world of man's inhumanity to man. *Oh, God. Without you, man is worse than an animal. There is absolutely no hope.* We viewed picture after picture of the atrocities in Nazi Germany and read stories recorded in journals and diaries. I wept, unashamedly, along with so many other tourists that day. I wanted to cry out to every Jew who didn't understand the difference between a Gentile and a Christian, "**Real** Christians love the Jewish people. Through you came the Word of God and our Messiah. The men who did those things didn't know Jesus."

*"Ye are the children of the prophets, and of the covenant which God made with  our fathers, saying unto Abraham, And in thy seed shall all the kindreds of the earth be blessed. Unto you first God, having raised up his Son, Jesus, sent him to bless you, in turning away every one of you from his iniquities."* (Acts 3:25,26)

Bethany, Bethlehem, Nazareth, Capernaum, Jericho, Masada, the Jordan River, the Dead Sea, the Sea of Galilee - all became *real places* - and we could envision the patriarchs of old and our Lord Jesus as they walked where we were walking. It was an experience we'll always cherish.

### Athens, Greece  April, 1988

"Pick any place in the world, and I'll take you there for our thirtieth anniversary in April!" Jim offered. He had just received an inheritance check and felt the Lord's urging to bless me.

What an offer! The world atlas became a constant companion over the next few days. *Where do I want to go? I had visited Europe in my teens and Israel in recent years. We've seen almost all of the United States. I know! An inland cruise in ALASKA!*

"I'm sorry, but Alaskan cruises don't exist in April, Mrs. Stone. You can go on one only in the summer." The travel agent quickly eliminated the only inspiration I had.

Back to the atlas. Australia? Japan? Scotland? No, none of those places seem right.

Finally, I remembered to ask, "Lord, where do **you** want us to go?"

*Go to Athens, Greece, and don't make any plans.*

Athens? That wasn't even a consideration in my perusal through the atlas. The impression was so strong that I announced to Jim, "I prayed about where to go on our trip, and it looks like Athens, Greece, is it. We shouldn't go on a tour though. I think the Lord said to go there and not make any plans."

A week before our scheduled departure, a lady and her husband with whom we had recently become acquainted were having dinner with us. We talked about our upcoming trip to Greece.

"Would you mind if I call a friend in Oregon and give her your name? She has a daughter in Athens and is really concerned about her soul."

"Sure it's okay," I answered. "The Lord chose Greece, not me."

In a few days, a very excited woman called from Oregon. "I called my daughter, Christine, in Athens, and asked her if she'd be willing to meet you. She told me to have you call when you arrive." Giving me her daughter's phone number, the woman went on to tell me how long she had been praying for her American daughter and Greek son-in-law.

We arrived in Athens on Good Friday evening. The next day, I called Christine. She was anticipating our call.

"How would you and your husband like to attend an Easter sunrise service at the Acropolis?" she asked. "It's for English-speaking people."

"We'd love to!" I exclaimed.

"Meet me in the lobby of your hotel at 5:45 A.M. tomorrow morning."

Even our tiredness from the long plane trip couldn't dampen our spirits. At 5:30, we were in the lobby, ready and eagerly waiting. It wasn't hard to find each other! At that hour on a Sunday morning, no one else was around.

It was still pitch dark out when the taxi let us out at the foot of Philopappos Hill. When we reached the top, we stood in hushed silence waiting for the first signs of daybreak. As soon as it was barely light, Christine, pointing to another hill, informed us, "That hill over there is Mars' Hill."

In my imagination, I traveled back over the centuries and pictured the apostle Paul standing on that very hill preaching his bold sermon.

*"Then Paul stood in the midst of Mars' Hill, and said, Ye men of Athens, I perceive that ye are too superstitious. For as I passed by, and beheld your devotions, I found an altar with this inscription, TO THE UNKNOWN GOD. Whom, therefore, ye ignorantly worship, him declare I unto you"* (Acts:17:22,23).

From Philopappos Hill, we had a magnificent view of the Acropolis. Leaders from many of Athens churches participated in this ecumenical service. When it began, we were impressed to find many reciting the Lord's Prayer in their own languages.

Here we were in Athens, standing on a hill once sacred to the mountain nymphs, gazing at the Acropolis dedicated to the goddess Athena. Nearby stood Mars' Hill, dedicated to yet another god. I felt grateful that Paul brought the true and living God to this city, and today we could stand here with our brothers and sisters in Christ and celebrate the resurrection of His son. We were encouraged to say, "He is risen!"

at the first sign of sunrise. We did, and the officiating pastor responded, "He is risen indeed." How wonderful to know the risen Christ. My grateful heart was overflowing.

After the service, we walked through the old part of the city and stopped at a coffee shop for pastry and coffee.

Arriving at Christine's home, we met her husband, George, who spoke very little English, and his cousin Nikos, who spoke a little more. Both men did their best to make us feel welcome. It was so nice to share a meal in a Greek home rather than in a restaurant. Christine prepared *spanikopita* (a spinach dish made with feta cheese and spinach, with a crust of philo dough). She also treated us to *dolmathes* (grape leaves stuffed with flavorful rice). Everything was delicious!

As Christine and I visited, we found many things we had in common, such as sewing for others and a love for cooking. When our discussion turned to spiritual matters, she listened intently as I shared the reality of Christ in our lives. Then I told her how we happened to come to Greece, specifically Athens, with instructions to not make any plans. Tearfully, she recognized that our time together was ordained of God, and she shared her heart with me. Because we had no schedule, we were able to spend many quality hours together.

When we left Greece, Christine again reassured me that our trip had been specifically for her. We had spoken many things from scripture that she had needed to hear at this point in her life. There was such a supernatural bonding that in the next year, Christine visited us in New York.

An excited Christine called from Greece recently to share all the good things that God has done in her life since the week we met in 1988. She thanked us for being obedient to the Lord by coming to Greece to share Christ with her. The joy of the Lord was apparent as she told of the people she has led to Jesus, her involvement in a ministry to children, and her participation in a women's Bible study group.

I once saw a brochure for a Christian summer conference that said, "Plan a vacation with a purpose." When we allow God to be our travel agent, He plans our vacations with **His** purpose in mind. We go where He wants us to go and meet whom He wants us to meet.

*"Also I heard the voice of the Lord, saying, Whom shall I send, and who will go for us? Then said I, Here am I; send me"* (Isaiah 6:8).

## Chapter Twelve

## Acknowledging Him as Realtor

*"All the commandments which I command thee this day shall ye observe to do, that ye may live, and multiply, and go in and possess the land..."* (Deuteronomy 8:1).

### Lake Park, Florida   May 12, 1979

"Mom and Dad, the people whose lawn I mow want to know if we're interested in selling our house. They have friends moving down who love our yard."

This somewhat surprising announcement from Jeff coincided with our repentance at not leaving Florida a couple of years ago (Chapter 7). The idea of selling our house without long months, or maybe years, of potential buyers peering in closets and criticizing my choices of wallpaper or carpet colors was very appealing. It had been a difficult time for me when we had tried to sell the house in 1977.

Our house wasn't just a house to me. It was our "dream home," and so much of myself went into every corner of it - from helping Jim design the plans to every facet of decorating. It also held fond memories of the many church meetings and corresponding activities that happened here.

My mind drifted back to some of the humorous events, too. "Jim, remember the time Tim's pet snake, Corny, got out of the cage and we couldn't find him?"

"What I remember most was your reluctance to tell our cleaning lady, Phoebe, that there was a snake loose somewhere in the house!"

"Well, I figured if I **did** tell her, she wouldn't come; if I **didn't** tell her, I'd come home from my dressmaking shop and find her fainted dead away on the floor! Thank the Lord, opting not to tell her worked out okay! Corny had a six-week nap, curled up inside an end table. Then we found him, not Phoebe. That was one time I was glad she hadn't cleaned more thoroughly."

That event started us reminiscing about stories of our kids' experiences with animals. Jim asked, "Remember when Tim and his friend Tony found the civet cat?"

"Remember? How can I forget?" I answered. "I had been out grocery shopping and the whole area reeked skunk when I turned into our driveway."

Tim and Tony had seen the Florida skunk in our yard and decided to catch it. The animal climbed a small tree to evade its pursuers. Tony climbed up after it while Tim ran into the garage to get a cage. Eventually they managed to trap the civet cat and brought the cage onto our screened-in porch. All the while, the frightened animal did what comes naturally! The boys managed not to get sprayed, but everything else in the path did.

Horrified when I realized that the odor was emanating from our porch, my vow not to yell at our children was quickly forgotten. "**Get that thing out of my house!**" I shrieked.

The boys gingerly carried the cage to the far edge of the back yard. Before turning the civet cat loose, Tim decided to take a picture. He circled the cage, looking for just the right the angle. The civet cat was looking for just the right angle, too. Just as he lifted the camera to shoot the picture, the animal lifted up on its front legs, aimed its rear end, and shot an odorous stream right up Tim's nostril! All we saw from the porch was Tim diving head first into the sand. "Ow! That burns!" he yelled.

"What about the time our dog Ginger, trying to get out to the kids, tore out all fifty-three feet of screen on the porch?" I asked.

"That wasn't so funny," was Jim's glum reply.

Our reminiscing ended, and the conversation turned to selling our house. I offered to call the woman who had spoken to Jeff, and she said, "Establish a price and I'll see if my friends are interested."

We had no idea of the market value and called a realtor friend. "Julie, could you do us a favor and appraise our house? We think the Lord is about to sell it, and we have no clue as to an asking price. While Julie was there doing the appraisal, she told us about a deal her company was offering and asked if she could list the house. After praying, we decided to "try God," and let Julie list it. We had several stipulations - no FOR SALE sign, no one could show the house except Julie, and we couldn't leave until September.

My prayer was, "Lord, you know how difficult it was for me to show the house the last time. There can be only one buyer, so please send that one."

As it turned out, we never heard from the friends of Jeff's customer.

The following are entries from Jim's journal:

**May 31, 1979**
"A young couple with five children came to look at the house. They were moving to Florida to work at Pratt and Whitney Aircraft.

After they left, SanDee commented, 'They're nice! They can have my house.' "

**June 2, 1979**
"Julie came to discuss the offer made by the people who looked at the house a couple of days ago. It was generous, and we signed the contract. SanDee can't believe how easy it was. God's time to sell was now, not in '77."

There was no "FOR SALE" sign, Julie showed the house to the **one** buyer, and we could close on September 7. The incident with Jeff's customer happened so that we could line up with God's method and timing for selling our home.

A side benefit of selling the house was an answer to a three-year-old prayer of Jim's. One day he was reading **Romans 13:8**. The first part of the verse jumped out at him. *"Owe no man any thing ....."* Although not in context, the Lord spoke to his heart through the verse. *It's time to get out of debt.*

"Lord, I'm **willing** to get out of debt, and you're **able**. You'll have to show me how," was Jim's prayer. When he left RCA, the only remaining debt we had was the mortgage on our house. Intellectually, we couldn't figure out how to repay such a large sum. Now, occasionally, Jim would pray, "Lord, I'm still willing to get out of debt."

When Julie appraised the house, it had appreciated to almost triple what we had invested in it. Perhaps this would be God's answer to Jim's prayer. We had never considered leaving Florida, or this "dream home," before now. We envisioned living here forever and watching our future grandchildren climbing in the live oak tree in the front yard.

When the excitement over the easy sale of our house waned, it suddenly occurred to us that we'd be homeless in three months. Our prayers intensified. "Lord, please show us where you want us to move. We know it's out of Florida, but please direct our path."

### New York  July 25, 1979

The gasoline shortage was getting much publicity. We considered delaying our trip to New York to get Terri, a girl graduating from the Walter Hoving Home. We had offered her a home and promised to attend her graduation. Our plans were to take her back with us when she completed the program. Not wanting to disappoint her, we decided to trust the Lord to get us there. We knew that He was well able to lead us to the necessary fuel supply.

Once we drove out of Florida, we began to ask the Lord to show us where our future home would be. We liked north Georgia and North Carolina. "Here, Lord?" we asked. No answer.

We visited some friends in Hagerstown, Maryland, and thought, *Maybe here?* Still no answer. Jim jokes that he stopped praying after that! He had lived most of his life in Florida, and he was sure we'd continue to live in the South.

While we were at the Walter Hoving Home, one of the graduates invited us to meet the people who had opened their home to her and her three boys. Two families in Milton, New York, were living together in an old resort hotel. They had a ministry to children and had several adopted and foster children as well as some of their own. Sandie was to regain custody of her boys. They had been taken from her because of her former drug habit. She was asked to live with these families as she adjusted to her new life in Christ.

Loryn encouraged us to visit. "You'll like these people, Mom and Dad. They even have church in their home!"

We felt an instant rapport with the one couple at home when we arrived. We shared about our present predicament. "In September, we'll be homeless and we have no idea where the Lord wants us to go."

Mike and Mary Jeppsen listened thoughtfully, then Mike suggested, "Why don't you move here and  become part of this ministry?"

That short visit was destined to change our lives. New York wasn't even a consideration in our minds. We were willing to go where God wanted us to go, but...New York? *Lord, you really wouldn't send us to New York, would you?*

We had dinner with both families that evening. We lightly tossed around the idea of our moving to New York. As we were preparing to leave, I jokingly said to Mary, "Find me a two-story house with a fireplace, and we'll come!"

She immediately responded with a twinkle in her eye, "I know just the house!"

Neither Jim nor I could sleep that night. We knew the Lord was saying,  "New York is where I want you."

As soon as morning came, Jim asked me to call Mary. When she answered, I told her, "We were scheduled to leave today, but the Lord seems to be prompting us to move to New York. Make an appointment and we'll look at the house you mentioned."

That afternoon we returned to Milton and looked at the house. I didn't like it at all. It had two stories and a fireplace but was so ordinary. I knew I had to be willing to accept it if this was the Lord's will. There was a contract pending on the house. We went ahead and submitted an offer anyway. Secretly, I hoped the house would sell to the other people.

When we arrived home in Florida, we learned that the house we looked at had been sold. It seemed that God used that episode as an impetus to prepare us to move. Now that we were convinced of His will,

Jim and I arranged to fly back to New York. We scheduled **one** day to find the house He had for us.

Mary had arranged for a local realtor to show us the available homes in Milton, and Marlboro, the next town south. A ladies' prayer group was meeting when we arrived at Mary's, and we asked them to pray as we house-hunted. The realtor showed us a few houses, and I got depressed. They were either too expensive or in terrible condition if in our price range. Anyway, none seemed to feel right. Jim knew we had to pay cash for a house with the proceeds from our Florida home. God had shown him a way to get out of debt, and he would take it. It would have been ludicrous to pray for three years and then deny His answer. Our price range severely limited our choices.

The realtor dropped us off after exhausting all of his resources. The praying women were eager to hear our report. "Nothing was right," I informed them, "but we still have a few hours left."

Casually glancing at the local newspaper on the table, I turned to the classified ads. A realty ad caught my eye:

"HIGHLAND:   Estate sale. Victorian farmhouse."

Turning to Mary, I asked, "Where's Highland?"

"It's the next town north of here," was her reply.

For some reason, I felt excited about this ad. Calling the listed realtor, we arranged to meet him and see the advertised house. He drove but was negative all the way there. "You won't like this house," he warned. "It needs a lot of work. An 89-year-old woman had lived alone in it for years and made no improvements."

Soon he turned in a winding driveway. Through the 100-year-old pines sheltering the front of the house, I caught a glimpse of a peaked roof. In a few seconds, I saw a large bay window in, what turned out to be, the dining room. *This is it!* I thought.

Jim was sitting in the front seat of the car next to the realtor. I was alone in the back. Jim looked over his shoulder at me, and we nodded in agreement to each other. We both instantly knew this was the right house before we ever set foot in it.

The realtor saw only the work involved, but we saw the potential for restoring this once-grand house. It was even more than that. We felt the approval of the Lord. I'm glad we *both* did, because the first winter was a real test of faith. We almost froze! The antiquated coal furnace, which had been converted to burn oil, was very inefficient.

We offered the amount of money we knew we would have from the sale of our home in Florida, and the owners accepted it. They probably knew it would be a difficult house to sell, but the price was perfect for us.

On September 10, 1979, we arrived in New York. Our furniture was already stored in the house. An acquaintance of the Jeppsens, a driver for Allied Van Lines, offered to arrange a delivery to Florida. He then took our household belongings back to New York and charged us only for gasoline. Our son Jeff rode with him and helped unload all our earthly belongings before we arrived. When we finally allowed the Lord to be in control, everything fell into place.

Our previous three years in Florida made us think of the children of Israel and their forty years in the wilderness. We were grateful that our lesson was learned in three. We were about to enter the "promised land."

*"And it shall be, when the Lord thy God shall have brought thee into the land which he swore unto thy fathers, to Abraham, to Isaac, and to Jacob, to give thee great and goodly cities which thou buildest not, And houses full of all good things, which thou filledst not, and wells digged, which thou diggedst not, vineyards and olive trees, which thou plantedst not, when thou shalt have eaten and be full; Then beware lest thou forget the Lord, who brought thee forth..."* (Deuteronomy 6:10-12a).

When we arrived in New York that September, we found succulent grapes growing wild along the edge of the property. A garden had been planted by a grandson who was guarding the house after his grandmother died. Tomatoes and zucchini flourished yet. Grandma's heirs left many usable items in the house. There were canned goods in the pantry and a bathroom closet full of unopened bars of soap. It was a year's supply for everyone living with us! Another closet stored candles of every variety imaginable. In the basement, we found over a gallon of pure Vermont maple syrup. The attic, barn, and garage yielded an abundance of treasures. There were old diaries, the first school board minutes of our county, handwritten in 1839, and many collectible items.

One time when we didn't have money, Jim discovered a pump handle in the garage. Curious, he pumped and gasoline came out. We used it to run our car for quite some time.

The first spring brought treasures of another kind. One late March day when my thin Florida blood thought it couldn't survive another minute in a cold, drafty house, I opened the back door. There on the frozen ground, I saw a patch of green, resplendent with tiny white flowers. *Maybe spring really will come,* I thought.

Those tiny snowdrops began a succession of flowers of every description. Out of that cold, brown earth, a profusion of colorful flowers began to pop up daily. Following the snowdrops came purple and yellow crocuses. Soon, starting at the back door and continuing down a garden path to the side of the house, red tulips, pale cream-colored narcissus, and sunny yellow daffodils bloomed. Throughout the spring and summer, we were to enjoy violets, wisteria, lilacs, forsythia, rhododendron, roses, poppies, peonies, iris, lily-of-the-valley, day lilies, tiger lilies, and flowers I never could name. To think, I didn't plant one of them! Our wandering was over; we had come out of the wilderness and entered the promised land. God's promise to Israel became ours. We would not forget the Lord who brought us into the land.

*"Behold, I make all things new..."* **(Revelation 21:5a).**

I began to understand certain scriptures in a deeper and more meaningful way than ever before. In Florida, where the seasons are so much the same, I missed many examples that the Lord gives us to appreciate in nature. Each **visible** earthly example is given to teach an **invisible** heavenly truth.

I thought of Jesus' words in **Matthew 6:28-30** as I looked at the lilies in our yard: *"Consider the lilies of the field, how they grow; they toil not, neither do they spin, And yet I say unto you that even Solomon, in all his glory, was not arrayed like one of these.*

*Wherefore, if God so clothe the grass of the field, which today is, and tomorrow is cast into the oven, shall he not much more clothe you, O ye of little faith?"*

The lilies were so beautiful, yet God cares more for our needs. *Thank you, heavenly Father, for taking care of us. We, who were created in your image, are so much more important to you. Help us to always trust you.*

That first spring in New York taught me new depths of understanding about death and resurrection. It was such a miracle to me to see flowers resurrected from the seemingly dead earth, but how much more a joy to contemplate the resurrection of Jesus Christ, and of each human being who experiences the new birth He offers.

We lived in that house for nine years. It proved to be exactly the place the Lord chose for us. It was wonderful to trust Him as realtor, He who can see the future as well as the past and present.

When we originally moved to Highland, Jim had no thought of pastoring (Chapter 4). We were sure our ministry would be solely to people in need of a Christian home. Again and again we saw how shortsighted our vision was. The Lord knew that He would lead Jim into a pastorate again, and He provided the barn on our property - ideal for the church meetings of Canaan Fellowship.

We never expected to leave New York. After nine years spent in restoring our home, we had settled in forever, content to enjoy the fruits of our labor. God has a principle in scripture though - move, when He moves, to stay in His blessing.

When the children of Israel were in the wilderness, God led them with a cloud by day and a pillar of fire by night. Only when the cloud moved could they move on. Until then, they stayed in their tents.

*"At the commandment of the Lord the children of Israel journeyed, and at the commandment of the Lord they [encamped]; as long as the cloud abode, there the children of Israel pitched their tents"* (Numbers 9:18).

*"Or, whether it were two days, or a month, or a year that the cloud tarried upon the tabernacle, remaining thereon, the children of*

*Israel abode in their tents, and journeyed not; but when it was taken up, they journeyed"* (Numbers 9:22).

### Arkansas May 1987

"Let's go for a ride and look at some of Arkansas," Jim suggested.

We were on vacation visiting our son Tim and his wife, Karen, who were living in Siloam Springs, Arkansas. Tim had been hired as an illustrator for Dayspring Cards, a Christian greeting card company in that city. Karen was also employed by Dayspring, and we spent our days alone while they were at work.

We headed north into a more mountainous region. Seeing a FOR SALE sign pointing up a steep, country driveway, we decided to see what real estate prices were in the area.

Ironically, the owners of the house were from New York! Because of health problems, they felt the necessity to move back to "civilization." This area was pretty remote.

We chatted for a while, looked at their house, and left. As we drove back to Siloam Springs, we talked, our excitement growing.

"Could you believe that all that acreage plus a house was only $57,000?" Jim asked.

"Why don't we look at other properties while we're here," I suggested. "Maybe Mike and Mary would be interested in moving to Arkansas. You've been talking to Mike about the value of moving his growing family to a less expensive and more rural area. This sure meets both criteria!"

That started a real estate searching adventure, with Mike and Mary in mind. A realtor in Siloam Springs suggested we contact a realtor in Huntsville for acreage. We looked at the Arkansas map to find Huntsville. It was a small town about sixty miles east. Jim called and made an appointment to look at some land there.

The realtor took us in his four-wheel-drive vehicle over some beautiful and wild terrain. By the third piece of property, we temporarily forgot about Mike and Mary and began to think about us! This property was beautiful! It was 59 acres on top of a mountain, with a magnificent view from every side.

"I'd love to have a log home right up on top!" I exclaimed.

"We don't buy anything we can't pay cash for," Jim explained to the realtor. "If we ever get some money, you'll hear from us! I doubt if the owners would accept what I could offer now," he joked, reaching into his pocket and holding out a handful of change.

Two weeks after we returned to New York, Jim received an unexpected inheritance check from his mother's estate. Holding it out, he asked me, "What should we do with this?"

"You told the man in Huntsville that he'd hear from you if you ever got some money. I guess you should call him. It isn't quite what they were asking but call and see what happens."

Jim called, and the owners accepted our offer. Suddenly we found ourselves  Arkansas property owners!

(We brought real estate brochures back to Mike and Mary, and they visited Tim and Karen that next year to check out the land. Circumstances worked in their lives that allowed them to precede us to Huntsville!)

**May 1988**

By this time, a year later, memories of our property in Arkansas were vague. "Guess we should go back and check it out," Jim said. The property was as beautiful as we remembered. We wondered what we were going to do with it.

On the way home, we both felt a desire to move to Arkansas and build a log home on top of the mountain. Logically, it made no sense. The church in our barn was thriving, Jim had a job that would pay a small pension if he left after 1990, and we were just about through with our restoration efforts on the house. I wanted to sit back and enjoy it after all these years of hard work.

The feeling of wanting to go to Arkansas persisted to such a degree that we began to pray for the Lord to show us His will. Was His cloud preparing to move?

### June 1988

I answered the phone, and a man's voice announced, "Mrs. Stone, this is David Wilkerson. I'd like to come look at your house tonight at 6:00 p.m."

"Really! Who **is** this?" was my reply, sure it was a prank call.

"This **is** David Wilkerson (The Cross and the Switchblade). I'm calling from New York City." He mentioned a mutual acquaintance who had told him that we were considering a move to Arkansas." I'd really like to look at your home tonight."

"But it isn't even for sale! We're just praying about **when** to go to Arkansas."

"I'll be there at six o'clock tonight."

Finally I agreed, thinking, *We asked the Lord to show us if and when we should move. It seemed crazy that a well-known and respected man of God would drive 70 miles from New York City in rush-hour traffic to look at a house that isn't even for sale!*

At 6:00 p.m., David Wilkerson really did show up. We took him on a tour of the house and barn and then sat on our deck sipping lemonade as we talked. The house wasn't what he had in mind. He expected it to be in a more rural and less trafficked area. We honestly didn't care one way or the other. According to our logic, it wasn't time to move anyway.

Before David left, Jim mentioned that he had no idea why we were moving to 59 acres in Arkansas.

"I do," was David's reply. "I think it will be used as a haven for people who will flee the east and west coasts." Then, at Jim's request, he gave us some advice. It made us perk up and listen. "Sell this property by January 1989, and go to Arkansas."

January 1989? That is a year too early.

In the days to follow, we knew we had asked God to show us if we should move to Arkansas. Now an uninvited guest whom we had never met was telling us to move a year before we thought we could, or should. If this was God's answer to our prayer, we didn't want to disobey, but we wanted to be sure. Orlando was an ever-present memory of what it was like to not be in God's perfect will for our lives.

Jim suggested the following list of criteria for selling the house:

1.    We would not list with a realtor but completely trust God to play this role.

2.    We would not put out a FOR SALE sign.

3.    We would sell only to Christians who would continue to keep the property dedicated to God.

4.    We would ask for a down-payment large enough to pay cash for our log home in Arkansas.

5.    We would carry the mortgage so that we had an ongoing income in Arkansas.  This would give us the freedom for Jim to not have a full-time job.

6.    We would not leave before the end of March 1989 so that we could move without bad winter weather.

Jim laughed, "I feel as though I'm acting like Elijah, pouring barrels of water on the altar **(I Kings 18:17-40).** If the Lord allows us to sell the house with all these stipulations, I'll know it was His time for us to move."

Certain phenomena began to occur. Many of the young couples in the church made a geographic move farther north, to avoid the steeply rising prices in the Poughkeepsie-Highland area. God raised up leaders within that group, making moving the church a distinct possibility.

We had the house appraised by several realtors so that we'd have an idea of what to ask for it. To our amazement, the property had appreciated five times what we had invested in it nine years before. One realtor told us that a house and property of this size and value would take at least two years to sell. Jim replied, "We don't have two years. We have to sell it by next January."

"May I list it?" the realtor asked.

"No, we decided to list it with the Lord," Jim answered.

A minister heard we were thinking about moving. He called and asked to look at the house. "Your house would be perfect for a ministry to boys. Would you consider holding it for us for a month while we try to raise the necessary funding?" We were willing to do anything at that point, and readily agreed.

A woman who worked with Jim at the Department of Social Services mentioned our house to a man she knew, and he called. He was a non-believer and was looking for a house and workshop for his business. Ours sounded ideal to him, but he didn't sound ideal to us. We had asked for a Christian to buy the house and continue to use it for God's purposes. It was good to be able to say that we had a contract pending on the house. Of course, he would have thought us crazy if he knew no money had changed hands. A verbal agreement between Christians was all that we needed.

Less than a month passed when we were released from our promise to hold the house. The funds were not readily coming in for the ministry to boys. God allowed that episode to happen just at the right time to protect us from an otherwise embarrassing situation.

**November 1988**

A woman called me one day and introduced herself as a Korean believer. She went on to tell me, "A group of us in the Korean church are feeling led to start a new work. The Lord told us to buy your property."

"But you've never seen our property. I don't even know you!"

"Well, a lady from your church mentioned that you were praying about leaving New York. She and I worked on a retreat weekend team, and I did see your barn. Remember when the team borrowed it for meetings?" I did remember. We weren't involved, so we never met any of the team members meeting there.

"May we come to look at the property this weekend?" she asked.

That Sunday afternoon, three Korean couples showed up at our home. We took them on a tour of the house and barn. We couldn't understand a word of their conversation with each other (They spoke in Korean). Their stoic expressions didn't give us a clue as to what they were thinking.

An hour later we stood in a prayer circle in the living room. Jim, called on to lead in prayer, asked for the Lord's will to be done in both our situations. Upon completion of his prayer, one of the men said, "We will buy this property."

Jim told them the asking price and the need to have enough cash down to build our house in Arkansas. It was a sizable amount of money, and we were amazed to find that the men were not only in full agreement, but excited.

"Let me explain," one of the men offered. "Two of us entered into a financial investment that we thought was of the Lord. As it turned out, it wasn't. We told the Lord that if we could get our money back, we'd invest it in His kingdom. This week, we were reimbursed for the total amount. It's exactly what you requested as a down payment!"

Now we joined in their excitement!

The house was sold by January 1989, just as David Wilkerson had suggested. The Lord did it without any help from us!

On Easter Sunday, March 26, we attended the dedication of the Korean church. The church would meet in the barn and the pastor's family would live in the house. We couldn't have found more dedicated Christians to continue His witness in that neighborhood.

*"Now unto him who is able to do exceedingly abundantly above all we could as or think, according to the power that worketh in us, Unto him be glory in the church by Christ Jesus throughout all ages, world without end. Amen"* (Ephesians 3:20,21).

Mike and Mary found a comfortable little house for us to rent while our log home was being built on the mountain. On February 5, 1990, we moved in. It seemed important to us to name the property, and we prayed for a suitable one. SHEPHERD'S HAVEN was the name we felt God gave us. Now we are waiting to see what He is going to do with it.

Many times since we moved to Arkansas, we have had to remind ourselves that God is never in a hurry, but He is always on time. As

Jim prayed about God's future plans for us and Shepherd's Haven, the only answer he seemed to get was, *You're in place.* One thing for sure, the place we always want to be is in the center of His will.

   *"Rest in the Lord, and wait patiently for him..."* **(Psalm 37:7a).**

## Chapter Thirteen

## Acknowledging Him as THAT NAME

*"Wherefore God also hath highly exalted him, and given him a name which is above every name"* **(Philippians 2:9).**

"When God spoke the world into existence, Christ was there." Jim and I were attending an evangelistic service in West Palm Beach, Florida, a short time after we were married. The speaker began his message with this thought, and it sent a thrill through every fiber of my being. I sat spellbound for the rest of the service, as he went through the whole Bible and told who Christ was in every book. For my first few months as a Christian, I mistakenly thought that Jesus began His life as a baby in a Bethlehem manger! Now, this man was proving that He always existed. He was there when God created the world and will be there throughout all eternity.

*"For by him [Jesus] were all things created, that are in heaven, and that are in earth, visible and invisible, whether they be thrones, or dominions, or principalities, or powers - all things were created by him, and for him; And he is before all things and by him all things consist"* **(Colossians 1:16,17).**

Understanding this concept early in my Christian experience convinced me that I couldn't leave Him out of any area of my life. The revelation of who Jesus is, recorded in the pages of scripture, has continued to govern my life. Jesus Christ, as the eternal Son, existed before all things, created all things, and by Him all things hold together. How **could** I exclude Him from anything?

I can still remember the excitement when I saw that Jesus was with the Father from the beginning. In Genesis, the Hebrew name for God, *Elohim,* is used. The very first sentence says, *"In the beginning God [Elohim] created the heaven and the earth."* The name *Elohim* is a plural word. It is used again when God talked to *someone* about the creation of man. *"And God [Elohim] said, Let us make man in our image...."* I believe He had a conference with His Son. What a thrill to discover that I was created in His image, and God's will is to conform me to the image of His Son **(Romans 8:29).**

As the years have gone by and I've walked the path of life God has chosen for me, I've often thought about Jesus **always** being there. Surely this *Unchanging One* would be there with me, as He was with the three Hebrew men in the book of Daniel as the fourth man in the fiery furnace.

*"And these three men, Shadrach, Meshach, and Abednego, fell down bound into the midst of the burning fiery furnace. Then Nebuchadnezzar, the king, was astounded, and rose up in haste, and spoke, and said unto his counselors, Did not we cast three men, bound, into the midst of the fire? They answered and said unto the king, True, O king. He answered and said, Lo, I see four men loose, walking in the midst of the fire, and they have no hurt; and the form of the fourth is like the Son of God"* **(Daniel 3:23-25).**

In the midst of my fiery trials, He was there. When I had cancer, He was there. When Loryn's husband divorced her, He was there. When we thought Tim and Jeff were lost on the mountain in Wyoming, He was there. He promised His disciples after His resurrection that He would always be there.

*"....lo, I am with you always, even unto the end of the age"* **(Matthew 28:20).**

In **Proverbs 18:24,** He is my *"Friend that sticketh closer than a brother."* When my earthly family rejected my faith in our Messiah, He was there to be my friend. What a comfort to know that **nothing** can separate me from His love **(Romans 8:35-39).**

I've been continually amazed at the analogies to a shepherd and a lamb that scripture gives us concerning Jesus. In **Psalm 23:1,** He is my Shepherd, providing for my needs as I learned to seek Him first. Acknowledging that I am the sheep and He is my Shepherd has kept me in a protected place. He has then been able to lead me to green pastures as I feed on His Word. In the wonderful messianic passages of **Isaiah 53,** He is pictured as the Lamb brought to the slaughter - the sacrificial lamb bearing the sins of many. In **John 1:29,** my Shepherd became my Sacrificial Lamb who took away the sins of the world, and more specifically, my sin, as I acknowledged Him as my Savior so long ago. Knowing that I am forgiven is a constant source of peace. In **John 10,** He is the Doorway to salvation; the Shepherd who knows His sheep and protects them from the predators who would seek to kill and destroy.

How could I ever have imagined all that embodied the wonderful, matchless name of JESUS, when as a Jewish teenager I dared to say THAT NAME.   In **Isaiah 9:6,** He is called Wonderful, Counselor, Mighty God, Everlasting Father, and Prince of Peace. In **John 14:6,** He is the Way, the Truth, and the Life.

In the fifteenth chapter of the gospel of John, I learned so many valuable lessons. Jesus is called the True Vine. As long as I remain a branch, abiding in that vine, I will draw my strength and sustenance from Him. By abiding in the vine, I will bring forth much fruit (v.5), I will have my prayers answered (v.7), and I will be called His friend (v.14). He is my Refuge, my Fortress, and my Deliverer. He gives angels charge over me, keeping me safe in all my ways **(Psalm 91).** He is the Lamp to my feet and Light to my path **(Psalm 119:105).** If I stay close to Him, He will illuminate my every step on this pathway through life. In **Hosea 2:15,** he replaced my Valley of Achor (trouble) with Himself, a Doorway of Hope. In **1 John 2:1,** he is my Advocate. If I sin, He will intercede before God for me. He is the Author and Finisher of my faith **(Hebrews 12:2).** Is it any wonder Jesus says, *"Without me ye can do nothing?"* (John 15:5).

When I took the name Christian, I accepted all the responsibility that goes with it.

*"Thou shalt not take the name of the Lord, thy God in vain; for the Lord will not hold him guiltless who taketh his name in vain"* (Deuteronomy 5:11).

I used to think that taking the name of the Lord in vain was to use His name as profanity. *I'd never do that as a Christian!* How ignorant! Taking His name in vain is expressed to others every time I fail to exemplify His life in me.

One time my mother worked with a professing Christian. She somewhat emphatically informed me one day, "Ellen isn't a Christian."

"Why do you say that, Mom?"  I asked.

"Because she gossips and loses her temper all the time," was her reply.

Well, that lady's salvation was based on her faith in Christ, but her actions and attitudes certainly took the name of the Lord in vain. It made me want to represent Christ to the world - not in my righteousness, but His. We are the only Bible some people, including my mother, will ever read.

The name of Jesus represents everything that He is. Someday, every person who ever existed will recognize Him as Lord of Lords and King of Kings. However, that recognition has to happen in this life to be eligible for *heaven. How grateful I am that I made that choice.*

*"Wherefore, God also hath highly exalted him, and given him a name which is above every name, That at the name of Jesus every knee should bow, of things in heaven, and things in earth, and things under the earth, And that every tongue should confess that Jesus Christ is Lord, to the glory of God, the Father"* **(Philippians 2:9-11).**

In 1986 a poem was written by Roy Lessin to promote a new line of Dayspring Cards. Sometime later, our son Tim set the poem to music. The title of the song is "Fingerprints of Love." The theme of the song is my prayer and desire for every reader of this book. "Jesus, God's hand extended, touching every aspect of our lives - leaving fingerprints of love."

I've tried to share every aspect of my life in Christ and hope that your life will be imprinted with His love as you acknowledge Him in all your ways.

If you've come to the end of this book and your innermost being longs to know Jesus, I have good news for you. He is no respecter of persons. You, too, can take that first step in acknowledging Him as your Savior. I invite you to pray this simple prayer. This decision doesn't mean that you'll be free of problems or heartache along the path of life you walk. It does mean that Jesus will be with you - guiding, comforting, protecting and loving you every step of the way. He really does make all the difference.

Dear God:

I accept your evaluation of me. I know I have sinned and need your forgiveness. Thank you, Lord Jesus, for giving your life for me on the cross to pay the penalty for my sin so that I could be forgiven.

Right now, I turn from going my own way and choose to have you come and take complete control of my life. I will acknowledge you in all my ways and trust you to direct my path.

I pray this in Jesus' name  - -  **THAT NAME!**


Signed_____


Date_____